D1189026

How to Become an Alpha Male

The Lazy Man's Way

to Easy Sex and Romance

By John Alexander

Copyright Notice

Now, let's get on with the good stuff.

Praise For "How to Become an Alpha Male"

Delivers the value promised...
"The fear I always have is that a book won't match up to the sales buzz created on the promotional site but your Alpha Male guide certainly delivers the value that you promised. I scanned through it and was very impressed by how thoroughly you covered many topics that truly define the alpha male... dress, etc. "
– Mike Pilinski, Author, *Without Embarrassment: The Social Coward's Totally Fearless Seduction System*

One of them gave me a blowjob...
"I tried your techniques tonight and had two chicks approach me right off the bat. The night ended when one of them gave me a blowjob...while the other set a date with me for next week!"
– Ken S., Miami, FL (from email on 01/02/2005)

"The most insightful material I've ever seen...very solid stuff"
– Brent M., La Jolla, CA (from January 2005 email)

Sex with college professor...
"I'd been fantasizing about my twenty-something college professor for two semesters, but she couldn't even remember my name. 8 days after I got your material she handed me a note asking me to stay after class. When I got to her office she locked the door and practically raped me!"
– David K. (from email on 03/10/2005)

"Of all the dating guides available, hands-down yours is the most valuable..." – Phil R., Yonkers, NY

"The things contained with your guide, I feel, are going to change my life... All of a sudden women are looking me dead in my face with this "longing look" and then smiling…."
– Tyrone P. (from email on 04/13/2005)

Table of Contents

Foreword

Congratulations on your purchase. "How to Become an Alpha Male" will make an amazing improvement in your life. The system I'm going to reveal to you absolutely works, and if you apply it, you **will** get laid.

How This Product is Different

Though I completed this book in June 2005, I began writing in 2003 because I'd read every "how to pick up girls" product out there and found that, although many were good, often they were too damned difficult for the average shy guy who's never had much success before.

I'm not saying that those systems don't work, because they do. The problem is that guys don't need to memorize laundry lists of "do this" and "do that" in order to get a girl.

Basically there are two types of products out there:

> 1. **"How to Seduce" guides.** These focus on using psychological methods to captivate a woman's imagination, often using hypnosis, and in the process lead her to have sex with you.

> 2. **"How to Attract" guides.** These focus on displaying attractive traits to a

woman, such as using humor, busting on her, telling stories, giving snappy answers to her questions, having her see that you're a popular guy, etc.

Do you notice an underlying similarity between these two methods? Both focus on the **woman**. Because of that, there's a huge list of stuff that you must do in order to get laid. It's burdensome!

So I'm introducing is a much easier system. Instead of focusing on the woman, "How to Become an Alpha Male" focuses on **you**. That way, you can simply become a guy who women think is hot, and then, merely by being yourself, find easy sex and romance.

Having said that, however, I'm going to also teach you everything you need to know about the psychology of women, what makes you into an attractive guy, and what you should do and say to get non-stop streams of women.

My system is the easiest because it's based on improving yourself rather than worrying about what the girl thinks, memorizing attraction-building routines, hypnotic patterns, and whatnot.

The bottom line is that you can get sex without going through stress or hassle. This stuff isn't rocket science. All you need to do is... **Become an Alpha Male**.

Introduction

I'll bet you think that since I'm the successful author of a very popular dating book (namely, the one you're reading right now), that I'm a born stud who's never had any trouble getting women. Yeah, right...

You know that guy you went to high school with who just didn't have it in the social skills department? The guy who couldn't get a date on a bet? The guy who was awkward to talk to because he couldn't even hold up his end of a decent conversation? I was that guy.

Throughout high school and early college, I had no friends, didn't hang out with anyone, and struck out with every woman I dated. I spend my Friday and Saturday nights alone, sexually frustrated. My 21st birthday came and went, and I was still a virgin. I was miserable and I didn't know how to change that.

To make matters worse, I took my failures personally. I figured there had to be something fundamentally wrong with me, and because of that, I felt deeply depressed.

I didn't like feeling like that, and refused to accept that the situation was hopeless.

So I decided to do something about it. Success with women was a skill that I saw other guys having, and I was determined to learn what they knew.

Over the next few years, I went to work.

I went out of my way to make friends with guys who were successful with women and I copied the things they did. I read psychology and communication literature to the point that I could swear I knew more about some of it than college psych professors knew. I worked obsessively to improve myself in every way imaginable, from my attitude to my physique.

To learn how to talk to women, I got up my nerve and talked to scores of chicks. And even when I struck out, I learned from the experience.

And you wanna know what? It paid off. I devised the system I'm going to teach you, and ever since I figured it out you would simply not believe the success I've had with women.

I'm not a geeky kid anymore—I'm pushing forty. And I can honestly tell you I've fulfilled my dreams as far as love and sex are concerned, and I'm happy in every way you could name.

Like I said, I read enough about psychology and communication to make me an expert in some areas, and I've hung out with some of the most successful men around when it comes to women. But you don't have to go through all that, because I've condensed it down for you to just the nuts and bolts.

This book is a distillation of everything I've learned and used to become successful. Not only that, but the information I'm going to share with you is stuff I've used to train other men to become successful.

So as you embark on your own journey toward self-improvement as a man, **assume that the advice you read in this book works until proven otherwise**. In other words, ya gotta have faith!

This book lays it on the line for you as to what women find attractive in a man and shows you step-by-step how you can not only **act** in attractive ways but also actually **become** an attractive man. And when you **become** an attractive man, you'll achieve your dreams just by being yourself.

A personal note to those of you who might be thinking: "Yeah, sounds great, but I am who I am and that ain't changing." Bullshit. Change is in your mind. As you imagine, so you shall be. Ninety percent of being successful is believing you can be successful. We're talking mental image here, which is a technique that almost all top athletes use. They visualize themselves being successful.

Think about this for a moment: let's pretend you just won the lottery, won big. You've got a million bucks. If you were to walk into a club tonight, do you think you'd walk more confidently? Project yourself with more authority? Sure you would! Chicks always know when a guy's got something going for him, be it money, power, or whatever, just by the way he handles himself.

And I'm going to show you not just how to handle yourself, but how to truly be more confident, so that your walk and talk practically scream to the world, "Hey, I AM the shit!"

CHAPTER 1: The Truth About Women's Love of Sex . . . It May Surprise You

"Women are too complicated"
"Women are too needy"
"I don't understand women"

You hear that crap all the time. And, honestly, it's a cop-out. Other men say that because it's easier to throw up their hands and just relate to women as black boxes that can't be understood than to try and wrap their minds around understanding women.

Here's what you need to understand about women, and it's good news: they are very sexual creatures on a fundamental, biological level. In fact, they probably enjoy sex even more than we do. Ever notice how women moan during sex much more than men do?

What All Women Live In Fear Of (and the trick to soothing this anxiety so they'll do whatever you ask!)

Unfortunately, society conditions women to believe, in the logical portion of their minds, (not the emotional portion) that it's "wrong" to enjoy sex.

Because women tend to be social creatures (more so than men, for reasons of evolutionary psychology), **labels such as "slut" or "whore" have a strong, negative effect on them**.

None of these penalties apply to men who have lots of sex. Thus, the supreme tragedy of the misogynistic system set up by religion and society to repress women's sexuality is that men everywhere have more of a challenge in getting sex than they would if they were living back in pre-civilization times when women were wild and uninhibited.

So your job as a man in modern society is to get around a woman's societal conditioning and draw out the natural woman within her.

Sound hard? Believe me, it's not! In a way, women are like padlocks. They seem impossible if you're using the wrong keys, but once you find the right key, they open easily. And yes, you CAN do this. I'm going to show you how.

To draw out the natural woman that lies deep inside every chick, you must always bear in mind that **on a subconscious level, women love sex and they want it just as much as (and maybe more than) we do**.

And as if the societal conditioning that women are subjected to isn't bad enough, a much more powerful force lies within them: their biology. A perfectly natural consequence that can result from having sex is having babies, and every woman knows it.

And she knows that if she gets pregnant when she isn't supposed to be pregnant, people will talk.

Therein lies the supreme tragedy of women; despite loving sex, they can't be free with their sexuality without being labeled a slut.

So while you--as a sexual man--move your encounters with women towards sex, you need to prevent her from feeling like a slut.

(By the way, it's to your own advantage to be discreet with women. The last thing you should ever do is be like the approval-seeking beta males who brag to their buddies about the women they've bedded. You don't need the approval of your buddies, so skip the locker room talk! Real men don't need to do that.)

Ever talked with guys who tell you, "We men will never understand women"? Well, women really aren't as mysterious or hard to understand as guys think. Nor are they as different from us as some of us might think.

Since we know that women want sex, it's OK for you to have sex as your agenda when you interact with them. In fact, it's actually a good idea.

What you should avoid doing at all costs, however, is **verbalizing** your intentions. You do NOT want to say anything about sex, or your intent to have it, to the woman.

Whenever you reveal your sexual intentions to a woman by saying something about it, you engage the logical portion of her mind, which causes her societal conditioning to kick in. "Uh oh," she thinks.

"This guy is tacky, gross, and creepy. And I could end up being a slut here."

So avoid being explicit about sex, and keep in the back of your mind how much women love sex, and work on **projecting** sexuality without saying anything at all about it. Use your body language, not your mouth.

What Women Like

Don't listen to what women say when they talk about the kind of men they like; instead watch their behavior and look at the kinds of men they actually go for.

If a woman were honest, she would say that the type of man she likes is "a sexual man who will create an opportunity for sex and will persist past my barriers." She doesn't dare say this, however, because she's terrified of some calling her a "slut."

Women like relationships, but that's not something they need a man for. After all, women have very close relationships with their female friends. I can't repeat it enough—women want a man who provides them with good sex.

And here's another biological bummer: women usually assume the passive role when it comes to sex. So that means that you, the man, need to take responsibility for the sex by pushing the encounter steadily towards the lay.

Don't make her take the lead. I mean, think about it: she lives in fear of the slut label **and** you're expecting her to initiate sex? It's no wonder so many guys have trouble getting laid. That's way too much to expect—a woman's simply not going to go out on a limb that much.

For you to get laid, you're going to have to create a situation where the woman feels like she can have sex with you without consequences for her.

For example, last month I picked up a woman at happy hour. We talked for a couple hours, about the topics I'll reveal later that make women super chatty.

We hit it off well, and then (two hours into our conversation!) she tells me that she has a boyfriend.

At this point, there were a number of ways I could have reacted. Most guys would have either:
    a) Gotten upset and left, feeling bitter about how the woman had "led me on."
    b) Tried to talk themselves up and convince the girl to dump that other guy for them.

Most guys would have opted for either a or b. Believe me, I used to do that too. Instead I've learned that the best thing to do is what I call "Option C": react nonchalantly, maintaining my alpha male composure and demonstrating that what she said didn't phase me.

"Good," I said playfully. "He'll keep you occupied when you're away from me."

She laughed, which meant it was fully on between her and me that night.

I don't normally go for chicks with boyfriends, but she'd been flirting hard with some guy in a bar for two hours, so how good could that relationship be?!

(And by the way, if a woman comes onto you who's in a relationship, mark my words... if she doesn't have sex with you, then she'll find some other guy to hook up with and satisfy her carnal desires. Her current boyfriend is unsatisfying to her or else she wouldn't be flirting with other guys.)

As the evening went on we had the perfect excuse for her to swing by my place. She was a big aficionado of the British Royal Family, and I told her about my collection of gossip magazines from the time I vacationed in England. "Come check them out," I said.

Once we go to my apartment, of course, it was just a matter of me maintaining control of the interaction and allowing her to slowly heat up sexually. (I reveal how to do this in a later section of this guide.)

Around 2 AM she decided to leave my place, not wanting to spend the night. All she'd wanted from me was sex, with no strings attached. (She knew that no one would ever find out about what she and I did.)

In other words: sex with **no consequences**. That's what women crave.

You've probably heard about women on vacation looking for out of town flings. Ever wonder why they do that? It's because there's no accountability for them; they're not going to get called a slut. Sex happens spontaneously, because the conditions are right. A woman thousands of miles from home can fulfill her carnal desires, and no one from her hometown need ever know.

Don't Explicitly Talk About What You're Going To Do

There's a certain mating ritual that humans do. It's like a dance, which lasts for a number of hours. The mating ritual must follow the proper steps in order for the sex to take place.

We guys have an unfortunate tendency of wanting to always clear the air and find out from the woman straight up what's going on, where everything stands between the two of you, and how she feels about having sex. This is a huge mistake.

Never verbalize anything about where you are in the mating ritual with a woman. Don't tell her explicitly what you intentions are. That's a logical, male thing to do. Logical things kill emotions, and emotions are **crucial** for a woman to have in order to be sexually receptive to you.

By not talking about your intentions concerning sex, you'll make it seem like the two of you had sex spontaneously. You'll keep the emotional part of her engaged, while the logical portion of her mind stays disengaged. And that's good—it's the logical part of her mind that says, "No!"

If you come across to her as a real gentleman with whom she really hit it off, then she'll rationalize in her mind that even though she doesn't normally have sex on a first date, you were an exception.

Just remember: a good time for a woman consists of good sex with a man... and she wants you to take the lead.

CHAPTER 2: The Number One Dating Mistake Men Make and How to Avoid It, Once and for All

At the ripe old age of 23, a friend of mine got his first girlfriend. Even though he was just law student, barely getting by, he proceeded to spend over $3,000 on the girl in just one short, whirlwind of a month, blowing through expensive wines at restaurants and other unnecessary gifts.

Though he did get laid several times in that short time span, she left him for another guy. My friend was heartbroken for months afterward, not to mention that he had to get a part-time job to replenish his bank account.

Been there, done that. I've bought girls dinners, movies… even a $500 ring that I saved up for back in high school. It used to be that I'd routinely bring a girl a $30 bouquet of flowers on our first date.

All of that money spent, and not much to show for it. All I'd wanted out of the deal was to get laid. It seemed a really simple bargain... the chick would get the stuff I bought her, and in exchange all she'd need to do is spread her legs.

Sound familiar? Are you frustrated when you don't get laid like you should, after all the money you've spent?

Well, here's the thing: you're operating on a false assumption. Money spent doesn't necessarily equal legs opening.

The problem with lavishing money on a woman who hasn't earned it is what it communicates. And what it communicates to her, loud and clear, is that her value is higher than yours, so **you** need to earn her approval by purchasing it.

It's like you're saying, "OK, I know my value is less than yours, so how's about I throw in a dozen roses, an expensive dinner, and some really nice diamond earrings?" Get the picture?

The reality, however, is that if you know that your value is high, then you don't need to buy her approval.

I know that saying "don't buy things for girls" goes against what we men logically think, and it damned sure goes against what we're all taught. After all, we're all brought up to believe that if there's something of value that we want, we need to be willing to shell out what it takes to buy it, right?

Well, in the case of inanimate objects that don't think for themselves, that's true. But in the case of women, it's not true.

Consider the average super-hot woman. Most men regard her as highly valuable and thus they grovel before her and worship the ground she walks on. She walks into a place and her money's no good.

Yet what kind of dude does a woman like this typically go for? Usually one with high social status, who sees no need to buy her things in order to win her affections. Oh, sure, he does it later, after he has her, so that she has nice things to show off…but not while he's getting her.

The bottom line is that there are three unbreakable rules of spending money on women (screw these up, and not only will you go home broke, but with blue balls too). Always weigh whether to pay with these questions:

1) **What is my value and hers?** If you make a special effort to pay, you are communicating to her that you think she has a higher value than you.

2) **Has she earned what I'm going to give her?** As an alpha male, you reward good behavior. So make sure the woman has done something to earn your approval! (I recently lavished a $100 meal on a woman I'm dating. I did it because she has given me the world's greatest fellatio. Make no mistake about: **the one and only time** you should ever take a woman out on an expensive date is when she's done something significant to earn it, like pleasing you sexually.)

3) **Am I paying for this in an alpha manner?** Make sure to not frame it as you buying a woman into your bed, because that's beta and needy.

I want you to start getting a mental picture of yourself as a man of high value. Now, as a man of high value, you need to take the mindset that yeah, you're interested in the woman, but your interest is conditional upon her good behavior.

By the way, never **say** stuff to a woman things like, "I'm buying you this as a reward." Just reward good behavior and avoid encouraging bad behavior, and you'll find that things will work out better for you.

When you do buy the woman things, never make a big deal out of it. Say something like, "I'll pay for the coffee. It's no big deal." What that says to her is that you're more interested in the social interaction that the two of you are having and that you're barely thinking about the drink you just bought her.

It also means that there are no strings attached. By saying "it's no big deal," you make it clear that you're not putting pressure on her to reciprocate what you've done for her.

"Buying me things because he wants something later" is a behavior that many women consider manipulative and results in the man being denied sex. And to be quite honest, many men fall right into that trap by making a big production out of buying the woman nice things. Don't be that guy.

Unfortunately, the average woman has gone out with so many men who bought her things to try to get into her pants that when you start buying her nice stuff, it triggers an automatic negative reaction within her. "Eeew, he's trying to buy sex," she thinks, and then she turns off on you. The typical woman is not a prostitute and doesn't want to be treated like one.

Fine, but then what do you do when the check comes? Well, first off, you shouldn't take a woman out for a big, fancy date until **after** the two of you have had sex. Then, take her to an expensive restaurant as a reward for her good behavior.

Your first date should be something informal and **inexpensive** such as coffee. That way when the check arrives, it's really no big deal.

A basic rule of thumb is to ask yourself whether you'd pay if you'd invited out a casual male friend instead of that chick sitting across from you. If the answer is yes, then by all means do it.

And don't feel like you're being taken just because you picked up the tab for coffee. You don't want to lose a lay just because you were too stingy to buy a $3 latte.

The main thing you need to do is to realize why you're doing things. Never buy things for a woman or do favors for her because you think you need to earn her approval. Instead, adopt the mindset of the alpha male: anything you do for her is conditional on her having earned it.

CHAPTER 3: The Three Kinds of Men—Alpha Males, Beta Male "Nice Guys," and Jerks

The Beta Male "Nice Guy"

When I was growing up, my mom, aunts, and other older ladies always told me that to get a girlfriend, I would need to be a nice guy. I'd need to constantly buy a girl flowers, give her gifts, and take her out to eat.

"Wow," I thought, "I'll need to have a really great job so I can have all that money to spend!"

And unfortunately, I internalized their advice. All through high school and college, I tried to be the nice guy, the one girls supposedly wanted. Girls would always **say** how much they appreciated what I did, but the most action I ever got was a kiss on a cheek.

Then in college and beyond, the advice changed. All of a sudden it was common knowledge that to be successful with women, you needed to act like an asshole rather than a nice guy.

I tried that advice out and found that when I acted like a jerk, some women responded to me more. However, I still didn't get the success that I wanted. Though I did get to have my first sexual relationship, it was with a low self-esteem head case. And I still had problems with so many girls preferring other guys to me.

So I took a good, hard look at the guys who were successful with women, the ones who weren't, and the ones in between, and I figured out that there are really three classes of men. And there's definitely a pecking order as far as the women are concerned.

At the bottom of the list are the nice guys, who make up the majority of the male population. The nice guy is a man who basically pleads for sex. He shows up at a woman's doorstep with flowers, drives her to a fancy restaurant and buys her filet mignon with fine wine.

Then, after he takes her home, he gets blue balls because she doesn't even invite him in. And the hell of it is, he doesn't learn from this—he's back using the same tactics on the very next woman.

And you want to know what's really ironic here? Believe it or not, women consider nice guys to be manipulative.

It's quite obvious to the woman why the nice guy buys her so many things. "They're only after one thing!" is a common mantra that women repeat about nice guys. However, she thinks he might possibly have good relationship potential, so she may keep him on the backburner and eventually have sex with him.

And boy does she make him wait a long time! Some women set three dates as the minimum, which is like winning the lottery for the nice guy, since many other women make guys wait months until they "get lucky."

And when sex does come, it's a huge event and the woman makes a big deal about it. Hopefully the man doesn't have a high sex drive, because he won't be able to get sex whenever he wants. He's going to have to accept it on her terms when she happens to be in the mood.

So why don't nice guys succeed? The problem with the nice guy is that not only do women consider him manipulative, they also see him as **boring**. The nice guy talks about logical things like foreign policy or how a car engine operates. Sometimes he brags about himself and how much money he makes, implying that he can buy things for the woman. "How lame," she thinks.

Engaging in logical conversation and trying to impress a woman with your smarts and earning potential is a mistake that 99% of guys make. It kills a woman's attraction for you because it communicates **neediness** and **low value**.

If you weren't seeking her approval, you wouldn't be trying to impress her. If you instead were a man of high value (an alpha male), then she would be the one seeking your approval.

The other problem of course is that women who are engaged in the mating ritual with a guy absolutely loathe logical conversation. It snaps her out of her trance. So refrain from talking about that article on Chinese trade policies you read in *The Economist* until you're hanging out with your male buddies.

Don't misunderstand me, though. You should not pretend to be some kind of idiot around girls. In fact, women find it attractive when a guy is an expert in something. What you do, however, is make sure to talk about **interesting** things within your area of expertise, not mind-numbing things.

In fact, something you should begin immediately, if you haven't done this already, is to become an expert in something. It doesn't matter what... real estate, rock music, South Park trivia, religion, history, etc.

A man who's an expert is automatically an alpha male in that area. Just make sure to captivate her with the knowledge you share. Don't bore her. (When sharing facts, ask yourself, "Would this information be on 'Ripley's Believe It Or Not' or would it be something a dull college professor would say?)

Girls just wanna have fun, as the song goes, and the nice, boring guy ain't fun. Go to places where singles congregate and you can perform an interesting people watching exercise by checking out the couples that you see.

If the girl looks bored or is constantly chatting on her cell phone, then she's with her boyfriend. That's because her boyfriend is a nice guy who isn't playful with her and doesn't excite her.

If, on the other hand, she's laughing and looks like she's having a good time, then what you're seeing is most likely a pick-up attempt by an alpha male.

Notice, too, that the alpha male picking up a woman has an easy rapport with her. The two of them talk as if they've known each other for a long time.

The problem with being the nice guy is the mindset that it springs from. A man supplicating to a woman is doing it out of insecurity and desperation for her approval and sexual attention.

Want to lay hot chicks? Then keep this first and foremost in mind: The quickest and easiest way to kill any attraction a woman may be starting to feel for you is to feel insecure about yourself, or to be needy, or to seek approval. When you have the mindset of being desperate to please, you end up coming on too strong, too early. You become clingy. It's like you're begging.

There's an old saying about banks: they only want to loan you money when you're loaded already. If you genuinely need the money, then you can forget it.

The Problem With Being Her "Friend"

Have you ever settled for being friends with a girl, orbiting around her as the months go by, hoping she will eventually fall for you? Lots of guys do this, particularly the shyer ones.

These guys **end up acting as emotional tampons for women**. They listen attentively as their female friends tell them about what jerks the real men in their lives are.

Believe me, I've been there. The low point came when a female friend of mine, whom I had a massive crush on, wanted me to come hang out with her at her apartment. "Awesome!" I thought. This was the moment I'd been waiting for, right? Not quite …

We sat in her living room and like a nice guy, I followed her agenda, which included spending a good two hours meticulously going over everything that her next-door neighbor (a druggie bartender) said to her at lunch that day. "He laughed and called me silly. Do you think he likes me?"

I did the best I could—I told her I thought he was a jerk and that she could do better. I gave her all the legitimate, logical reasons why that was true. She told me she agreed with me. (Girls with the "wrong guy" always agree that he's wrong. Then, of course, they ignore it and have sex with those "wrong guys." As she did.)

If there's any justice in the world, eventually women will come around to liking the nice guys. Truth be told, sometimes they do, usually when they're older. By that point, they've usually already had kids by some jerk who bailed on them and the kids and the thought of settling down with a weak-willed man who will stick around and bring in a steady paycheck is starting to have an appeal.

Women just simply don't like spineless men for more than friends. And when you act like a nice guy and follow the woman's agenda, and defer to her to make decisions, she doesn't respect you.

Nice guys want the woman to decide where they go to eat and when they have sex. They have no clue that that deference automatically drops them down into the permanent "just friends" category.

And that's why the nice guy doesn't get laid. Like I said, women don't like to take responsibility for sex. You, as the man, need to take that responsibility and lead the way. That's what women want you to do, and believe me, they love it when you do!

Avoiding the Beta Male Mindset

In addition to being too indecisive, nice guys also tend to be passive-aggressive. Women are often being passive-aggressive themselves, thus they are turned off when that particular trait is exhibited in a man.

What's passive-aggressive? It's being passive until you've been pushed too far, then suddenly turning aggressive. Ever had a woman who expected you to read her mind and then got mad when you read it wrong? That's passive-aggressive.

Rather than hit the middle ground between passive and aggressive, which is assertive, the nice guy will constantly give in and do whatever the woman wants.

When the woman finds this unattractive and eventually leaves him for a more exciting guy, the nice guy will complain about how he "did everything for her." And therein lies the problem…

Nice guys also have issues with jealousy, born out of their insecurity. They are too outwardly-dependent; all their happiness comes from the woman. They don't want her talking to other guys for fear she'll run off and he'll lose his source of happiness.

You see, the problem with the feelings of jealousy that so many beta males have about their women is that it comes from a position of neediness. So whenever you feel that way with a girl, suck it up and let those feeling go.

When a girl detects a guy is jealous, it's as if he's saying to her, "Hey, I feel inferior to those other dudes you're talking to."

And having that lack of confidence in yourself makes the chick not feel so confident in you, either. She begins to wonder whether the grass is greener in other pastures.

I know it's tough to not feel jealous, but look at it this way: if you knew that you were the shit and that you can attract hot babes and get laid easily, would you care that your girl is going off and talking with some other guys? Of course not, because that would be her loss (and you could just get laid from some other chick)!

Okay, so here's a new attitude I want you to adopt: **"I am developing into a high value alpha male."** Keep repeating that to yourself throughout the day as an affirmation.

By the way, you're probably still wondering what you should actually do if you're girl is talking to other dudes. Well, the absolute worst thing you can do (ironically) is to try to intervene to stop her from doing it. That makes it so that she has the higher value, not you.

Instead, the best way to counter such behavior is to say, "Have a good time!" with a tone of complete indifference when she says she's going to go hang out with some other guy. Let her see that it doesn't phase you one bit.

Meanwhile, you go talk with other girls.

That turns the tables so that now she's the one worrying about whether you'll leave her for the competition. That sets you up as having the higher value.

Another way to avoid ever becoming upset at a woman's behavior is to not take individual women seriously or put much concern in what they're thinking.

Being overly concerned with a woman's thoughts and feelings is a waste of time, because the bottom line is **you can't control what a woman thinks or feels**. You can only control yourself.

Instead of taking women too seriously (which gives them power over you, making you needy and unattractive), just view them as collective sources of fun and pleasure in your life. That's it.

In order to a spine with women instead of being a pushover, I have something for you to try.

Next time you're with a woman, try to say "no" to her at some point. Saying "no" can be powerful with women. But do it in a soft way, like this:

Her: "Let's go rent a movie."
You: "No, not yet. Let's go in about an hour."

By saying no, you establish your authority and set yourself up as a challenge for the woman. If she views you as a challenge, then she will be excited by you instead of bored.

If you say YES to everything your woman suggests, then she will soon be saying NO to you, and in the worst place of all... the bedroom.

What you need to know, most of all, is that women resent any sort of neediness. The alpha male is exciting to women because his happiness comes from within, so he doesn't burden her with any responsibility for his emotional state.

Let me stress one thing here: your inner state is **key** with women. For them to see you as lovable, you have to first love yourself. You have to have passion for your life and you've got to go for what you want.

There are way too many nice guys out there who are down on themselves and insecure. That's why when it comes to love, nice guys really do finish last.

The Jerk

On a middle level, above the nice guy, is the asshole, or jerk. For the most part, assholes appeal to women more than nice guys because assholes aren't boring.

Though the asshole creates an emotional roller coaster of drama with his girlfriend, at least the girl is getting the emotional high points of the ride along with those low points. In other words, he may make her cry, but he also makes her giggle. And the uncertainty of which it's going to be does create some excitement in her life.

Here's what you need to get about women: **in order to be sexually turned on, women need to tune into their emotions instead of their logic**. The nice guy makes the fatal mistake of appealing to their logic, whereas the one good thing the jerk does do is to appeal to a woman's emotions.

Jerks get laid because they get women turned on by being so persistent and then going for the lay. They are sexually aggressive, unlike the nice guys who are sexually passive. While the jerk creates negative emotions within women, at least they are still **creating emotions**, as opposed to the nice guy who bores women.

However, it's not all good for the jerks. The types of women who go for jerks are mainly head-cases who have low self-esteem, depression and other emotional issues. Such women often act weird and insecure when it comes to relationships, so they're really not the kind of women a well-adjusted man would want to go for in any case.

Though jerks get laid, I'm not suggesting that you be a jerk. The good news is that there is a higher level of men yet, whom I call the alpha males, who induce positive emotions within women with no real negatives.

The Alpha Male

In society, alpha males are the leaders; people look up to them. The alpha male is confident, socially powerful, outgoing, fun, a leader, secure in himself, has high self-esteem, and is a guy who has his shit together. He's able to joke around with women and be playful.

When a woman says something sarcastic, the beta male gets offended, while the alpha male laughs about it because he knows girls are like his silly little sisters. And when a woman later regrets her sarcasm, and learns it was really no big deal to the alpha male, she gives him big points for that.

Many social interactions that we engage in have sub-currents of dominance and submission. Studies of social situations have shown that dominant people will mark their territory in various nonverbal ways, such as taking up space with their bodies, using a louder voice, controlling conversations, and using strong eye contact.

People around the alpha male tend to get sucked into his reality because he's interesting and makes them feel comfortable.

The alpha male doesn't feel possessive or jealous over woman because he isn't needy. He also doesn't smother women by putting them up on a pedestal. Because of this, he knows that any woman would be lucky to have him, so if any one particular woman doesn't go for him, then that's her loss, not his.

In contrast, the beta male is nervous, has low social status, is typically a follower rather than a leader, usually feels secretly resentful of successful guys, has low self-esteem, and is clingy and desperate with women.

True confession: I used to be beta. I was depressed and resentful. I wanted a girlfriend because I thought having one would make my life worth living. Once I got a girl and was able to have as much sex as I wanted, I thought, my life would become wonderful. It wasn't until later that I learned that I had this **exactly backwards**.

It wasn't until I developed myself from within and had a life worth living that I starting attracting the awesome girlfriends who I've had over the years and the wonderful woman who I'm currently in a relationship with.

In the next chapter I'm going to share with you some of my secrets on how **you** can affect the behaviors and mindset of an alpha male.

CHAPTER 4: 24 Nonverbal Cues That Scream "I'm Non-Dominant." Get Rid of Them and Score!

What do you think is the **one thing** that makes a man most attractive to women? It's the impression that you're a dominant man. And no, you don't have to grunt, scratch, and slap a women around like a cave man to convey dominance... nor should you!

You convey your dominant male status simply by acting the way dominant men do, by consciously controlling the nonverbal cues you send out, thereby creating the impression within a woman that you are alpha.

This technique is called the association principle. Within the mind of a woman, you're associating yourself with desirable masculine traits while dissociating yourself from undesirable "nice guy" traits.

This is how magicians operate. On stage, the magician carefully controls the audience's impression of him. By diverting the audience's attention towards things that they associate with magic—like his waving wand—he prevents the audience from noticing the thing that would make him look non-magical: the fact that he's using his hand to do the trick!

Similarly, you can use impression management to control what the woman thinks of you.

And here's some really good news: by adopting the proper mindsets talked about in this guide, you will eventually grow to fully become an alpha male. And you can start moving in that direction today by adopting the behaviors of an alpha male.

So what's dominance? It's social power, which comes from assertiveness. As you go through your process of self-improvement, eventually you will internalize the concepts of this book and **become** an alpha male.

Right now, you're going to learn how to **act** like an alpha male, giving the impression of dominance by using your voice, your eyes, your behavior and your posture.

Your eyes are the number one nonverbal cue that tells people you're an alpha male. A dominant man is not afraid to gaze directly at people. By averting your gaze, you communicate submissiveness. When you look down, you communicate self-consciousness, shame, and a sense of low status.

When you are the one talking, there is no limit to how much eye contact you can make. Studies have shown that the more eye contact the person doing the talking makes, the more dominant the listener perceives that person to be.

However, when you're the one doing the listening, the opposite is true: the less you look at the other person while they're talking, the more dominant you become. (Ever wonder why adults tell children,

"Look at me when I'm talking to you?" It's a way of reinforcing the adult's dominance over the child.)

Of course, you don't want to go overboard and have the woman think you're staring her down. If you're perceived as too dominant, then your likeability starts to suffer. So give your eyes a break every now and then. (In the next chapter I will deal with boosting your likeability.)

Another indicator of your dominance is your voice. Dominant people control the conversation. They also speak in a cutting voice and aren't afraid to interrupt the other person. Studies have shown that using a soft, quiet voice can give off the impression that you aren't assertive.

When you speak, try to let your words flow and don't be afraid to speak your mind. People who hesitate and hedge are perceived as less powerful than those who do not.

Watch your mannerisms and behaviors. Try to avoid the following non-verbal indicators of beta status:

1) **Using "ah" and "um," partial sentences, and partial words.** Studies have shown that people consider others who talk like this to lack confidence and not be too bright. It's a sign of nervousness. The reason we say "um" is because we're afraid we're going to be interrupted by the other

person. Instead, don't be afraid to pause for effect. Pausing before important points will make you seem more competent and people will remember what you say

2) **Speaking too fast.** This gives off the impression that you feel anxious and have low self-confidence. A normal, comfortable speaking rate varies within a moderate range from 125 to 150 words per minute. Slow down!

3) **Speaking with a monotone voice, also known as *mumbling*.** People with a narrow pitch range are viewed as unassertive, uninteresting, and lacking in confidence. So vary your pitch and you will be perceived as outgoing and alpha.

4) **Pausing too long before responding to a question.** This indicates that you're thinking too hard for your answer, which makes you seem indecisive. It also looks like you're trying too hard to win the other person's approval.

5) **Pulled-in, closed postures.** An alpha male spreads his arms and legs out and is open. When

standing, you can force open your body language by hooking your thumbs in your back pockets.

6) **Holding your hands in front of you.** This is a defensive gesture. Instead hold yourself open and vulnerable. (You hold yourself vulnerable because you feel no fear.) Let your arms relax and be open. Nobody's going to punch you, so why do you need to block yourself?

7) **Twitching your fingers or hands.** When you're across the table from someone there's a natural inclination to play with sugar packets or straw wrappers with your fingers. Don't. And don't drum your fingers on the table—women hate that.

8) **Touching your face when you talk.** This indicates that you're thinking too hard, you're indecisive, or that you feel shy. To convey confidence, hold your hands together in a steeple shape in front of your chest or face. (A lot of professors do this when they are lecturing.) Another posture that will help you when you need a huge display of confidence is holding your hands

at your hips. Cops do this when they need to establish authority over criminal suspects.

9) **Folding or crossing your arms in front of you.** On rare occasions it is possible to fold your arms in an alpha fashion (watch Brad Pitt in the movie *Fight Club* for a good demonstration of this), but as a general rule, avoid it.

10) **Rigid or hunched posture.** An alpha male has a relaxed posture, whether he's standing or sitting. Loosen up and spread out.

11) **Looking down.** The alpha man holds his head high. It shows zest. Looking down at the floor telegraphs "loser." Keep your chin up. Expose your neck— don't worry, nobody's going to choke you! Look at the person you're talking to; remember what I said about using your eyes.

12) **Nervous facial gestures** such as lip licking, pursing your lips, twitching your nose, and biting your lips. An alpha male has a relaxed face and mouth because he fears no one.

13) **Excessive smiling.** Studies of primates have shown that beta males will smile as a way to signal their harmlessness to stronger males. Beta humans smile to show they're not a threat. The alpha male, however, only smiles when there is something to smile about. And yes—he can be a threat.

14) **Walking fast as part of your normal walk.** Instead, walk a little slower than normal, almost as if you're swaggering. You're alpha—no one's chasing you and you're not rushing to please anyone else. If you're not in a hurry to get somewhere, walk like you're relaxed and confident. Think: "I am the man. I can make any woman happy."

15) **Walking only with your legs.** Don't be afraid to move your torso and arms. Try this: walk as if you'd just had a massive success and felt on top of the world. Watch what you do with your body. You may find yourself moving your arms along with your shoulders and having a slight bounce in your step. Now, do that all the time.

16) **Slouching.** You don't have to stand uncomfortably ramrod straight, but you should have your shoulders back. Watch Brad Pitt in any of his movies for examples of how to comfortably hold your back straight. (I keep bringing Brad Pitt up because he provides an excellent example of what good body language looks like. Also watch George Clooney. For fans of older movies, check out Sean Connery in *From Russia With Love* and Rock Hudson in *Pillow Talk*.)

17) **Blinking a lot.** Instead blink your eyes slowly. Don't close your eyes in discomfort. Just let your eyelids relax. In fact, let them droop a bit. Don't be bug-eyed.

18) **Shifting your eyes back and forth when you speak.** That's very beta. When you're in a conversation and you're doing the talking, gaze at the other person's face. Nonverbally, this communicates that that you say is important and worth listening to.

19) **Holding too much eye contact when the other person speaks.** Ignore the dating advice books that tell you to hold non-stop eye

contact. Non-stop eye contact makes you look needy, socially retarded, and, frankly, like a weirdo. Instead let your eyes blur and then *gaze* at her eyes. Look through her rather than at her. From extensive testing, I've found that gazing at a woman about two-thirds of the time is optimal. By the way, only hold the gaze when she's telling you something genuinely interesting. Otherwise, focus on other stuff like her breasts, her hair, things going on around you, etc.

20) **Being uncomfortable with your eyes.** The bottom line is that your eyes should be comfortable, relaxed, assertive, and sexual.

21) **Looking down or to the side before answering a woman's question.** If you do need to look away before answering in order to think, then look **up** and to the side. Studies have shown that this displays more confidence.

22) **Being afraid to touch a woman, and thus being non-touching.** Be confident about it when you touch women--any nervousness at all can be fatal for your relations with her. Be alpha

and physically move her when you need to. Hold her hand to lead her around, etc. Be gentle —if you use excessive pressure, you reveal your insecurity. (Since you're alpha, of course she will follow you, so there's no need to be anything other than playful and tender.) It's natural to touch others, as when you're emphasizing a point. So let the love flow!

23) **Turning your head fast when someone wants your attention.** Instead use the movements that you would when you're at home —slow and relaxed. You're not at anyone's beck and call. You're alpha, remember?

24) **Using long, convoluted sentences.** Alphas keep it short and to the point. If you're tempted to use long sentences, break them up.

Don't feel bad if you inevitably slip up and use some of these nonverbal cues from time to time. No one's perfect, so don't beat yourself up about it, especially when you're talking with a woman. Let it go and keep the conversation moving.

When you think about such things too much while talking, you start to doubt yourself, and when that happens, you feel insecure and anxious and become hesitant.   Instead just work on remaining nonchalant yet sincere at all times.

It's enough to simply **be aware** of how you communicate non-verbally with everything you do, because being aware means you will start to avoid negative communications much more.

CHAPTER 5: Six Beta Male Behaviors to Avoid

Here's something you may not know about us humans: we're wired to attach more weight to negative information about someone than we do to positive info.

That's why you can be having a great conversation with someone, and then all of a sudden you change your mind about them when they tell you in all seriousness that they were captured by a UFO.

It doesn't matter that for the past half hour the person was being smart and witty... now you mentally stamp their file with big bold red letters that say "WEIRDO" based on the UFO thing.

So, since one wrong move can shoot down 100 good ones, it's crucial to avoid negative behaviors that are characteristic of low status males, or betas, if you don't want women to treat you like crap and lead you on. These beta characteristics to avoid are:

1) **Seeking approval by ending sentences with, "isn't it" or "right"?** These questions tacked onto the end of sentences make you sound weak willed, particularly if your vocal pitch rises. Right?

2) ***Trying* to dominate. Instead, just do it.** Have a stronger psychological reality and mindset

than anyone else. Assume people are there to follow you, because you are the shit. Know, as an article of faith, that you can ask people politely to do what you want them to do, rather than bossing them around. (It's interesting to observe military generals, who, despite what you see in movies such as *Patton*, are usually polite when they get subordinates to do things.)

3) **Being belligerent, either with women or with other men.** The alpha male is able to stay calm under pressure and walk away when he needs to. Starting a fight is a sign that you're a man with low status. It also goes without saying that fighting in order to gain the affections of a woman is the ultimate form of approval seeking, which lowers your attractiveness. With that said, however, if some guy violates your boundaries and starts shit with you (like let's say you get bullied), there are occasions when you must stand up for yourself.

4) **Following the other person's agenda and talking about what they want to discuss, even if you find it boring.** Remember my story of sitting for two hours with the girl I loved, listening to

her tale of woe about the druggie bartender? Bad move. The alpha male only talks about what he wants to. Watch any alpha male in action (e.g., CEOs and politicians) and you will observe this phenomenon. When an alpha male is bored, he doesn't hide his disinterest. So don't give people your attention until they've earned it.

5) **Trying to one-up people and prove that you're smarter than the person you're talking to.** When you look at leaders in corporate boardrooms or governor's mansions, you find that the best leaders are secure enough in themselves that they can listen to those who are more expert than they are. An old CEO truism is that you don't have to be smart, you just have to hire smart people.

6) **Checking out every pretty girl you see.** A man who's getting laid left and right doesn't have time for this, so you shouldn't, either. As you stop being impressed by the hot bodies around you, watch the difference in reactions that you get from women. Watch how they start checking **you** out and wanting to prove themselves to **you**.

Alpha males assume the mantle of leadership as their birthright and act as if they are a natural leader. They don't care much about what others think. They do their own thing and don't seek approval.

However, at the same time, they also offer a benefit--whether it's social status, excitement, or stimulating conversation--to those who follow them.

People submit to the alpha's reality because they want to (since alpha males talk about interesting topics) or because everyone else is paying attention to the alpha male.

And people—especially women--pay attention because the alpha male conversation style is interesting. Why? Easy--because he talks about fascinating things. Thus, other people are sucked into his reality, so as a consequence they find them interesting too.

So how do you get interesting stuff to talk about? It's simple: you have an exciting, well-balanced life. If you do that, you will naturally exude attractiveness to women. Keep busy with work, your social life, activities, and self-improvement. Don't just sit around playing video games. Go skydiving, take dance lessons, call an old friend and hang out with them. When your life is fun and interesting, you have tons of things to talk about with women.

And when you talk to a woman, lead the conversation. Captivate her attention.

As you work on your behaviors, you will also work on adopting the mindset of an alpha male. The first thing I notice that all alpha males have in common is that they assume people will follow their lead. They're not bossy because they don't need to be—they have the confidence that comes with knowing people will follow.

Bossiness can quickly backfire because few people like to be ordered around. Do your thing and be passionate about it and people will be drawn into your reality. Just act as if people will follow you, believe that they will, and you'll find that what you believe will become reality.

This brings up an important point. Don't observe reality and then adjust yourself to it.

Instead, create your own reality. This means that you should act as if events are the way you would like them to be.

Act as if you are a catch for any woman. Act as if pussy is no big deal to you, since it's not a big deal to men who get laid all the time. (Although you may not currently have much sex, if any, you still want to model the mindset of men who do.) Act as if all your manly desires are perfectly natural. You have no reason to apologize for or cover up your sex drive the way nice guys do!

Act as if you're not affected that much by what a woman thinks, since what **you** think is a lot more important. Believe it or not, women will respect you a lot more for this.

Lots of guys get caught up in the trap of constantly wondering what a woman is thinking. "Gee, when she rubs her glass in response to me telling her a joke, does that mean she likes me?" Quit worrying!

Instead just realize that there's a horny, primal woman within her who wants to have mad, passionate sex with you. Just relax. Be an attractive guy, and give her a chance to become attracted to you. If she doesn't accept the gift of your companionship, then that's her loss.

Be optimistic. Ever notice how the best athletes such as Deion Sanders, Michael Jordan, and Tiger Woods **know** that they will do well? Success comes from confidence. Assume you will succeed, and your attitude will increase the odds that you will. Assume that you are irresistible to women.

Be powerful and resolute. But at the same time, be natural and fun. Be a bit of a bad boy, but don't be a jerk. Have a devilish smile on your face if you want. You're an exciting man and women should want you.

Do what you please in life. Be true to your emotions. If you don't want to do something, then don't. Be honest with yourself. Be your own man.

What does this mean? If you want to give a homeless man some change, then do it. If you want to help an old lady across the street, then go for it. If you want to open doors for your girlfriend, do it. Just don't feel like you have to do any of those things because it's expected of you. Do things because you **want** to do them.

In the end, when you become an alpha male, the man who is true to himself, you will experience the happiest time of your life. Getting laid will just be an aftereffect. How's THAT for a side benefit?

CHAPTER 6: How to Be an Alpha Male... When You're Taking Orders From Someone Else.

It's virtually impossible to be an alpha male yet follow someone else's orders. When you have someone telling you what to do, and you do it, you are the beta of that situation.

There are really only two ways to handle it, and both have their merits.

First, you can play the game. Do your job, take your boss's orders, make your steady paycheck, and hopefully you'll move up the corporate ladder. The disadvantages are that you'll have to play office politics to get anywhere, and your boss can fire you if you don't kiss his ass.

Situations like that are not the world's best for a man's sense of self-worth. And by the way, aggressive flirting with that hot secretary can get you fired. The guys in upper management don't like when lower level guys move in on their women. So do the bulk of your dating outside the workplace. (In fact, the best strategy at work is to always have the women work for you. That keeps you out of trouble.)

The second path is to throw it all away and start your own business. It involves a ton more risk, but at least you're in charge of your own destiny.

That's the path I chose at age 29, quitting the corporate environment to become an inventor, and I haven't looked back. I had some tough years financially, but I've done okay, later becoming involved in angel investment and venture capital. Money issues aside, the bottom line is that I take no orders from no one.

Be The Boss Somewhere!

Be in some kind of leadership position in your life. It doesn't matter if you're just a graduate assistant teaching a college class. Merely being in a position of authority **somewhere** turns women on.

Having your own business and being the boss of employees is an excellent situation to be in. Any time people are following you, you've got alpha status.

By the way, a fantastic place to have a woman meet up with is somewhere that you're the boss. One strategy for this is to say to the woman, "Come by my office, and we'll head to the coffee shop from there."

That way when the woman shows up, she'll see that you're the big man who people defer to, giving you the alpha male status.

CHAPTER 7: Project Your Ideal Self By Controlling the Way You are Seen

None of us truly live in reality. We live in what we **think** is reality, but it's actually just our own individual perception of what reality is. Ever cringe when you hear a recording of your own voice? Well, that's how others hear you. It's quite different from how you hear yourself, isn't it?

When it comes to the way they view you, people perceive you not as you actually are but as they **think** you are.

People project various qualities and traits onto you and then treat you accordingly. This can be either good or bad, depending on what their projection is.

The key point, however, is that once you understand that people project an identity of you, you can then take steps to control what that identity is.

A Basic Principle of Human Psychology That Successful Men Deploy to Get Women to Like Them

People are wired to want to keep their thoughts consistent with their actions. Psychologists call this the Commitment and Consistency Principle.

Once a person has behaved in a certain way, they **adjust their thoughts to be consistent with their behavior**.

In the 2004 US election, the Bush-Cheney campaign used this brilliantly by having attendees at its campaign rallies sign a statement affirming that they would vote for Bush. Having performed the action of loyalty, most attendees then adjusted their thinking in a way that favored Bush.

Signatures are only one such way that marketers use the Commitment and Consistency Principle to their advantage. Once a person has committed themselves with an action, they feel a strong need to justify that action to themselves.

From there, they behave consistently with the commitment they have made. No matter your view of politics, the Bush campaign did a good job getting highly committed grassroots supporters who were a force to be reckoned with, and those supporters turned out in droves on Election Day.

In most cases, the Commitment and Consistency Principle helps us as individuals. Life is so complex that we simply don't have time to process all the complex information in a situation if we've already done the same sort of processing in a previous situation.

Instead, we remember what decision we made before, and we stick to it. We think, "Oh, this is just like when such-and-such happened, and I did so-and-so." Then we proceed to do so-and-so.

For example, if you need to drive to a place that's in the same part of town that you work, you'll get in your car and take the same route that you usually take to work, rather than getting out a map to see if you'd save time by taking a side street.

Generally, this is beneficial since you'd probably waste more time by looking at the map than you would by driving a slightly longer route.

When it comes to interpersonal relations, people tend to project qualities onto us that jibe with the way they have treated us. If they do us a favor, they reason that it must have been because we deserved it, because we must have some positive qualities.

So, you should **never stop a woman from performing acts of generosity towards you**.

When she does a favor for you, she increases her good impression you by rationalizing to herself that you must be worthy of such good treatment.

To put it differently, always allow women to do things for you. If she offers to pay for something, let her. Never say, "Oh no, I'll pay for it." If she offers to cook for you, go for it. Don't say, "That's okay, I'll buy us a candlelit dinner."

Thank her and adopt the mindset that you deserve to have things done for you.

How to Compliment a Woman Effectively

Suppose a person really looks up to you. Is that, by itself, enough for them to like you? Probably not.

If your value is too much higher than theirs, they will get nervous around you and perceive that the two of you don't have good chemistry together, because they just don't feel very good about themselves when they're around you. This happens because they see you as **so much better** than themselves.

This is a problem faced by a lot of people who are perceived as "cool." Although they're seen as really cool people, others get stage fright around them.

As a consequence, a lot of cool people actually have trouble maintaining relationships (both sexual relationships and friendships.) So your coolness should be balanced by enabling the people you interact with to **feel good about themselves while in your presence**.

You're probably wondering, "How do you do that?" You do it by being free in giving out genuine compliments.

One way to do this is to make a flattering observation and then quickly ask a follow-up question in a querying manner, as if you're making sure that the woman is qualified to be with you. Remember, you are a good catch, so she will feel good when she impresses you.

Examples –
You: "You have an amazing energy about you. What do you do for fun?"
Her: "Blah blah"
You (thinking about it for a second): "Hey, that does sound like fun. I'd love to hear more about it."

You: You seem really cool. What do you study at school?"
Her: "Blah blah."
You: "Interesting! I have a friend who studied blah blah."

As you see, when you give a genuine compliment, quickly follow it with a question. This prevents the woman from denying the compliment and it also makes her prove herself to you.

In fact, she'll practically be eating out of your hand and believing anything you say as long as you make her feel qualified to be with you.

As an alpha male, you give approval without needing approval given back to you. So don't wait for her to thank you for the compliment.

Also, women commonly **deny** compliments, making them view themselves in a lesser light. And women may then think you gave out false flattery, which is the last thing you want. So don't give her the chance to deny your praise.

I like to follow up my compliment with a question, because then that sets up our interaction with the frame that even though I found something I liked about her, my approval can still be taken away if I don't like her answer. That puts me as the one with higher value, and it's her job to win my affections. She's then that much happier when she sees you're interested in her answer.

Now, here's something you need to watch: it's important that you don't give out fake compliments because then you're trying too hard for approval. Besides, it's tough to give a fake compliment and have it sound sincere, and you definitely don't want her to get suspicious.

Betas butter people up, alpha don't have to.

Another strategy I like, particularly with a new woman, is to quickly change the subject after complimenting her. "You seem really cool. Hey, you know what? On my drive over here, I saw . . .."

That keeps me in control of the conversation's direction, plus prevents her from having the chance to deny my compliment.

Another reason I like to sprinkle compliments in my interactions with people is that it keeps me externally focused. Because I'm thinking about them, I'm **not** burdened with worrying and over-analyzing my every move.

The Secret to Good Listening

Here's a dirty little secret: almost everyone is a little bit shy and self-conscious some extent. If they're talking to you because they think you're a person of high value (as a woman will think if she's attracted to you and making conversation), they will feel good if they believe they have **earned** your attention.

To instill in others the feeling they've earned your attention, look for the deeper meaning in what people are telling you. Once you've figured that out, address what they're really communicating.

Let's say someone says to you, "What percentage of our genes do you think we share with chimpanzees?"

What's the deeper meaning there? Superficially, they're testing your knowledge. But the real meaning here is that they're trying to show off **their** knowledge and amaze you with a cool fact.

Suppose you're a well-read guy and remember seeing something in National Geographic about how humans and chimps have about 98.5% of the same genes. Should you say, "98.5%"?

No. Alphas don't play other people's games.

A much better response would be, "I don't know, we couldn't be **all that** similar. Is it 50%?" The person will then feel like they have earned your attention when you tell them how interesting it is that it's 98.5%.

(If you feel like you need to display your intelligence, you're seeking the other person's approval and that's a sign that you have low status.)

Suppose someone tells you they just went to Panama City Beach. They say that because they feel excited about the trip they've just gone on and they want you to share in that excitement.

So the worst thing you could do would be to one-up them by saying, "Man, that's nothing. You should see the beaches and waves in Hawaii!" That statement shows you're indifferent to the other person and makes them feel like they're not all that special.

Instead, get them talking about the things they enjoyed about Panama City Beach. Say, "Sweet! I've wanted to go there. I'm curious; what was your favorite part of the trip?"

And even though alpha males interrupt when they need to, try not to interrupt people when they are talking about something that is interesting to you.

And don't worry too much about it when people interrupt you. People interrupt because they are highly involved in the conversation, which is exactly what you want.

When talking, be focused on **them** rather than yourself. Look at the reasons for what people are saying and then validate those reasons. This conveys your strong sense of inner contentment and makes you more attractive and likable in their eyes.

Genuinely think about what a woman says and be interested. Every girl is a new exploration, and you have so much to discover about her. So take your time in your conversations and be a good listener.

Two Magic Words That Reinforce a Woman's Good Behavior

Watch successful people and you find that they are more generous than the average person when it comes to saying, "Thank you."

When someone does a favor for you, they do it because they are framing you in a favorable light. By expressing appreciation to them, you legitimize their favorable projection of you.

Don't say things like "You shouldn't have" that indicate you didn't deserve what they did for you. A person gives things to you because they see you as being worthy of the best. If you kill this attitude of theirs, you convey that you're unworthy.

So whenever a woman compliments you or does something nice for you, never belittle it or ignore it. Instead, thank her with the full mindset that you deserved such nice treatment.

Remember—reward her good behavior!

By the way, whenever a woman compliments you, view it as her **really** saying to you, "I like you. I want you to keep pushing our interaction forward to the sex."

So say "Thank you!" and it'll almost hypnotically guide her into your bedroom!

Nine Nonverbal Cues That Say, "I'm Likable"

I've already listed non-verbals that convey dominance. There's some overlap—lots of those signals, such as sustained eye gazing while you speak, that convey dominance also make you more likable. However, sometimes dominance signals (such as leaning back) can make you more distant.

So where appropriate, you may need to balance your dominance with likeability. (Too much dominance makes you unlikable.) Be conscious of the following silent techniques that magnetically get a girl to you:

1) **Lean forward** when you're sitting across from someone who is telling you something. This communicates interest in what they are saying. However, it's crucial to make sure that the woman is highly interested in you before doing this, since leaning back is a way for you to non-verbally play "hard to get." Once she's interested in you, lean

forward to give the impression that you're easy to talk to.

2) **Directly orient your body and face towards her**. Note that you should have dominance established before doing this, since you lose dominance by being more direct with your body language.

3) **Smile**.

4) Have a **relaxed** and **spread-out** posture.

5) **Dress similarly** to your group, but just a little bit cooler than everybody else. If you meet the dress expectations of the people you interact with, you will be better liked.

6) **Wear lighter-colored and more informal clothing**. (However, such clothing also detracts from your perceived dominance.)

7) **Maintain mutual eye contact—go ahead and gaze into her eyes** and she will like you. Don't do it more than 70% of the time though, as stated previously.

8) Make sure your **speaking voice is pleasant, expressive, relaxed, and that you sound animated and interested** in what is being talked about.

9) **Avoid** unpleasant facial expressions, an absence of gestures, looking elsewhere,

closed body language, and an uncomfortable-looking posture.

Again, make sure to strike a balance between dominance and likeability. If you never smile, then the woman won't like you. But if you smile excessively, it makes you seem like you have low social status— you're trying too hard.

Some things such as a relaxed, spread-out posture help you with dominance **and** likeability, so you should be spread out and relaxed all the time.

Avoid conjuring up pity

A lot of guys make the mistake of trying to make a woman feel pity for them. They'll call obsessively, saying things like, "I'm so lonely and I really want to see you tonight."

On a psychological level, a lot of this may point back to the mother-son relationship. As little boys, we could often get what we wanted by evoking the maternal nurturing instinct in our moms.

Don't do this with women you date. Any time you evoke pity in a person, they will look down on you. In their mind, they'll frame you as a person who is a loser, and then they'll treat you accordingly.

Have you ever noticed that unsuccessful salesmen are the ones who appeal to your pity? ("Please buy this car so I can eat this month!")

Psychologically, people cannot help having derision for those they pity. The successful salesmen are those who make sure customers feel they (and not the salesmen) are gaining a benefit by buying their cars and not just feeling sorry for someone.

Avoiding the Big 3 Behaviors That Instantly Convey Low Status

Avoid the three behaviors below and you'll immediately separate yourself above 95% of the other guys out there. That by itself, when women sense it, immediately makes them feel wetter around you.

1. Bragging

"You should see my awesome house."
"I'm about to get a raise up to six figures a year!"
"I have a huge dick."

The irony of bragging is what it communicates —you're a needy guy who craves approval. Why else would you have to talk yourself up like that?

Avoid directly verbalizing your good qualities and let the woman discover them on her own. This displays your confidence in yourself as well as making you a bit "mysterious" in her eyes.

Be an endless source of fascinating discoveries for her, not a blowhard.

2. Putting yourself down

Lower status men tend to be modest for fear of offending others and because they want to be seen as polite. Alpha males avoid self-effacing modesty except when it's an obvious joke.

High self-esteem is attractive to women. Think highly of yourself and a woman will think highly of you.

It's okay to make an obvious joke about putting yourself down, like in the following examples (said with a playful tone of voice):
- "I'm so weak, I'm not sure if I can lift that heavy thing." – Spoken by a bodybuilder
- "I wear a leather jacket to compensate because my penis is so small. It's not even half an inch!" - Spoken by a man with huge confidence who obviously does not have sexual insecurities. (That's why he's able to joke about penis size.)
- "I'm unemployed and live in my parents' basement!" – Spoken by a well-dressed man who obviously has loads of money.

3. Putting other people down

"Ha ha look at that bum in rags!"

When you put down others, you reveal your own insecurities. The homeless guy on the sidewalk is no threat to you, so why act as if he is?

And since women are sensitive creatures who feel sorry for the less fortunate, you'll trigger her into taking up for whoever you put down.

Similarly, don't put down guys who are your sexual competition, since that too reveals your insecurity. Instead simply don't pay attention to them, since they're not worthy of your attention.

CHAPTER 8: The Most Important Power Attitude You Can Have

If you're like most guys, you think of women as a reward in life for working hard and living right.

It's a tradition going back in history. In the Middle Ages the beautiful maiden was the reward for the gallant knight at the end of his long, arduous quest.

Hey, I used to think that way, too. And it led me to believe I'd have to get the finest car, have the highest-paying job, and spend tons of money on women in order to get them to like me. All my friends thought that too.

The hell of it was, looking back, none of us had much luck with chicks.

"Man, if I just keep working hard and being a nice guy who knows just the right kinds of flowers to buy," I thought, "women will like me." After all, whenever you ask a woman for advice, that's what they tell you to do.

Later, I discovered that women give **terrible** advice! They provide you with the roadmap for becoming relationship material **only**. Take their advice and you'll be an easily controlled beta male who has to wait months before sex, as opposed to an exciting alpha male who women have sex with right away.

As a college sophomore, I had a huge crush on a female roommate of mine. I did the all the right things I thought I should do to get her to like me. I'd leave the toilet seat down. I'd buy her CDs. I'd fix things for her in our apartment. I even cleaned up after her when she'd trash the place.

I was such a sweet guy, she told me. But we never had sex. She never felt any attraction for me whatsoever. I was just...too...**nice**. And nice means **beta**.

Then during my junior year I made friends with a guy who seemed like the opposite of what I thought a guy should be like. He didn't spend money on girls, didn't eagerly jump to tag along with girls who asked him to go shopping with them, and didn't try to impress girls with his car or career ambitions.

Yet this man constantly had women admiring him, orbiting him, flirting hard with him, and having sex with him.

What he did, I later realized, was convey alpha male qualities that made women attracted to him on a primal level.

Everything about him and how he conducted himself reflected his wholehearted belief that **he was a good catch**. It was the power attitude from which all of his success flowed.

Because of his belief that he was a good catch, he:

- Would only have sex with women who had earned that honor.
- Would only feel affectionate toward women who had earned that privilege
- Would only be interested in what women said if they said something interesting and didn't just blather on.

Once you've completely adopted this mindset that **you are the catch** (not her), you will have become more attractive.

It's a fundamental part of human psychology that we tend to assign a higher value to things that aren't readily available.

That's basic supply and demand: whatever is in short supply is demanded at a higher price than usual.

As I write this book, for example, there's a reported market shortage of Splenda artificial sweetener. The company that makes it is trying to build a new factory because its current factory can't keep up with demand.

So now, thanks to news stories trumpeting that fact, people who never would have used Splenda in the first place are buying up months and years of the stuff.

Remember when they brought back the original Coke after introducing New Coke?

From rare baseball cards to stamps, there are examples of the scarcity principle all over the place. Marketers take advantage of it all the time.

As an alpha male, you can take advantage of this and increase your value through the following three secrets:

1) **Being unavailable to a woman if the benefit you'll gain is outweighed by what you'd have to put up with**. (If you take that attitude, how much patience do you think you'll have for women who put you in the "relationship" category and make you wait months for sex? Not much!)

2) **Not jumping to return phone calls so quickly.** As an alpha male, you're a busy man, and women need to earn your attention. And when you do talk on the phone, often you'll get off the phone first, not because some relationship book told you that you have to, but because you genuinely are a busy man

3) **Not being available for dates if you have other things you're doing with your life.** (And by the way, in order to be attractive to women, you **should** be doing things with your life other than chasing skirts.)

Let me say this again, because it's important— by not always being available, you will raise your value.

When you adopt the mindset that you are a high value man who decides for himself if it's worth his while to spend time with a woman, you will also have certain rules for behaviors that you will tolerate from her. When she fails to meet your expectations, you withdraw your attention.

As an alpha male, you live the life that you want, free from needing the approval of others. (Most people unfortunately do **not** live the life that they want for precisely that reason, i.e., that they're afraid of getting disapproval.)

Therefore, you move towards the things you want and away from the things you don't. You're a man of high value and are worthy of being treated as such by others.

CHAPTER 9: Creating Your Own Strong Reality

Your world is what you perceive it to be. On the internet, you can find a vast range of beliefs, and all of those beliefs are backed by people's own observations.

For example, many religious sites talk about God as if it's obvious he exists, while atheists say that's nonsense. Read further and you find compelling arguments for both views! How can that be, since both sides can't be right? It happens because each is a different person's view of reality.

What if you break your leg? Is that bad? You're probably thinking, "Damn right, it's bad." But let's suppose you're a British soldier in 1914 and that broken leg just prevented you from becoming cannon fodder on the Western Front. Then you'd thank your lucky stars for your leg cast and crutches!

So here's the thing: reality is what you perceive it to be. There is no objective reality. Everything is open to interpretation. How about if it's a rainy day? You'll have an entirely different perspective depending on whether you want to go on a picnic of if you're a farmer suffering through a drought, Even a flood isn't bad for everyone—people who kayak whitewater love floods.

Thus, you have the power to view the world the way you want to. You can have your own reality, your own frame on things.

A person with a weak reality gets drawn into other people's perceptions of the world. A person with a strong reality is unaffected by other people's perceptions, and instead draws others into **his** world.

Let's say you go to nightclubs and have trouble finding a place to park. A beta male who lets external factors control him will be upset by this. But you can frame it in a way that you don't have to be upset. Not being able to find a place to park means that there will be lots of people in the clubs, which means lots more women.

Ever get stuck in a traffic jam? That's okay, because it's a chance for you to take a break, relax, meditate, and maybe listen to some soothing music. You don't have to join the rest of the herd in becoming upset. You have the power to have a good perception of events.

Now let's look at what kind of frame you have when it comes to yourself. You want to have the frame that you are a prize that women will earn.

Easy Alpha Male Exercise – Fixing your mindset about yourself with women.

You need to **know** that every woman would be lucky to have you. Ponder the following questions. Come up with answers to them, and write down those answers.

This exercise may be easy, but it's important, because if you've not yet fully internalized the alpha male mentality, it is **essential** to redirect your thought patterns. Plus, it's always helpful to jot down a few things that you can later re-read when you need to be refreshed on your journey.

1. If you allow a woman into your life, how can you make her feel good in many ways?

2. Imagine you are a man of high value, whose time and attention are craved by lots of people. What are your rules for allowing people to receive the gift of your time and attention?

3. What are some fun things that you like doing that women also like? (Women need emotions in order to become sexually receptive, so they enjoy things that are **emotionally relevant** such as talking on the phone with friends. The easiest way to kill a woman's mood for sex is to talk about logical things such as corporate balance sheets.)

4. What are some qualities you have (or can develop) that women would find attractive?

5. What are some benefits you would need to get from a woman in order for you to bring her into your life?

Come up with your own answers, but keep in mind that there are certain things that women **must** have, such as great sex, passion, positive emotions, and sensuality.

While you provide benefits for women, you also want to screen them for quality. As a man, you probably have strong sexual desires (I certainly do!), so you would not want a woman who is frigid. For me, behaviors that will make me leave a woman are dishonesty, childish drama, and obesity.

The kind of woman I like is one who genuinely likes me, enjoys life, and takes care of herself.

Only you know what you want and what wonderful benefits a woman will gain by entering your world. I strong encourage you to complete this exercise before reading further in this guide.

Okay, now that you you've read the questions, thought about them, and written them down, you've now got your roadmap written out on how to become attractive and confident.

Put differently, you are on your way to realizing how special you are. In the world of love, you are like a Lamborghini. If a woman doesn't realize your value, then it's her loss, not yours.

I really like the Lamborghini analogy because of its relevance to a man's relations with women. A Lamborghini doesn't have inherent value—it can either be a hunk of metal that gets bad gas mileage, or it can be a thing of beauty and power that you would pay as much as a house for. It all depends on your perceptions.

Lamborghini dealers have a strong mindset that their cars are highly valuable. As a result, they don't just let anyone in for a test drive. They don't bargain with the price they expect to receive, unlike Ford or Chevy dealers who lack the high value mentality.

CHAPTER 10: The Simple Secret to Being Dominant

Dominance is the #1 trait that attracts women. What I'm going to reveal to you in this chapter will be the secrets that will have women begging to have "anything goes" sex with you.

Here's what it's all about: to be dominant, control the frame. It's as straightforward as that.

It is important to realize the importance of this whole concept of frames. As I've said, there is no objective reality. All reality exists in people's minds.

So if a woman creates drama that she thinks is a big deal, and you go along with that, then you have been reduced to beta male status by being sucked into her frame.

If on the other hand you reframe her drama as funny and silly and not that big a deal, then **she** has been brought into **your** reality.

To give an example from my current relationship, my girlfriend wanted me to go to her parents' house with her to meet them. I preferred to hang out with my own friends that night, so I told her those were my plans.

She reacted badly and said, "John, it's really important to me that you come with me."

Most men would get sucked into her frame by having a long discussion or fight over it. After all, you have long discussions about things that are important.

But if you frame it like her wanting you to meet her family is not a big deal, you'll simply react by saying, "Sure, let's do that sometime" and then quickly changing the subject to something more interesting. That's what I did, and it drew her into my reality.

Use that strategy that with everything. You as the man have the more powerful reality.

Because your strong belief system is now, "I'm a good catch" and "I'm the prize, not her," the woman will buy into that frame.

One of the jobs I held on and off for many years was part-time pizza delivery. (By the way, avoid eating pizza if you want to keep a trim waist!)

Back before I learned the proper mindset. I would always get incredibly nervous whenever I'd knock on a door and a hot woman would answer. This was because I considered them to be potentially great catches for me (rather than the other way around).

So when I tried to get them to like me, I came across as a guy who was trying too hard, which damaged any attraction the women may have had for me.

But then I adopted the attitude that I am a good catch. As a consequence, I felt **indifference** whenever I delivered to a hot woman. I would simply say, with a relaxed tone of voice and posture, "Hi. The pizza will be $X."

Sometimes women would *shamelessly* flirt with me as a result. (They **never** flirted with me before.) I had sex with a few of them, including one who I dated for over a year—she was absolutely amazing in bed. She worked hard to win my affections, because I was a challenge for her.

Women don't like to be put up on a pedestal. Even if sometimes women claim that they do, the men who actually are successful with women do not view them that way. They just act natural.

Women may be wonderful beings who want to have sex with you, but they put their pants on one leg at a time just like you do. When all is said and done, women are a lot more similar to men that most guys think.

The problem with putting women on a pedestal is that it comes from a frame of neediness.

Think of the people in your life who have been needy. They stifle you by trying to get your attention every chance they get. They constantly demand your attention, because they're seemingly unable to have a good time on their own.

Psychologically, this repels you rather than make you want to spend more time with them. So consider what it is like from a woman's perspective when you feel needy.

How can you avoid such feelings? Catch yourself whenever you have thoughts like:
- "If I lose this girl, I won't have sex for months."
- "I really want this girl to like me. What should I do to make her like me?"
- "Should I call this girl yet?"

The whole irony about wanting people to like you and trying too hard for it is that it has the opposite effect—it **pushes them away**.

So stop putting women up on pedestals. A better, healthier way to look at it is that **you** need to climb up on the pedestal yourself. You are the prize.

Take two examples of a man chatting up a woman. The first is a man who thinks he needs to earn a woman's affections; the second knows he is the prize.

Beta Male (nervously): "Can I please have the honor of taking you to lunch? It will be my treat. Where would you like to go?"
Woman: "Thank you!" (Smiles.) "I'd like to have lunch at the El Supero Expensivo Ritzo. Let's go!"

They go to lunch, the woman views him as a nice guy and a good friend, and he never gets laid because she just isn't attracted to him in that way.

And by the way, even though men complain about money spent on women in exchange for which they get nothing, women don't view this as them taking advantage of the guy.

After all, if you were put up on a pedestal and had someone nervously asking you to grace them with your presence for lunch, wouldn't you feel like you were giving them exactly what they wanted by doing them that favor? If a man has a secret agenda that the woman detects, then that comes across to her as creepy.

Alpha Male (relaxed and in comfortable in his own skin): "I'm off to get some lunch at my favorite place, El Cheapo Restaurant." (Then, playfully, almost like it's an afterthought): "You're a fun person, so come along with me."
Woman (giggling): "Blah blah" (It really doesn't matter what the woman says, because as long as she feels comfortable around the guy, she will go with him.)

Notice the frame that this second example sets. The man is in his own reality. He wants to get lunch and knows where he wants to get it.

Because the woman has earned his attention, she can come along with him. He is the prize, not her —she's fun, so she gets invited to come along.

In the first example, the woman is clearly the prize, as the man is weak-willed (doesn't have a place in mind to go eat), knows that his value is less than hers (so he comes across as nervous), and has to practically bribe her to talk to him.

Note also how "so come along with me" is really a **command**. You see, an alpha male is not afraid to put his balls on the line and say things like that to people.

Make sure, however, to soften such phrases by saying them playfully. You don't want to come across as harsh or bossy.

Finally, notice how lunch is not being framed as a date like it is in the first example. This avoids having her categorize the man as relationship material who will have to wait months for sex.

Instead, if sex takes place, he will assume the active role in creating the right conditions for it.

The way the mind works, as I mentioned earlier, is that when you believe something, your mind increasingly finds evidence for that belief to be true. That's the value of the above exercise for kick starting your belief in yourself as the dream lover that all women would want.

As you adopt the mindset that you are a good catch, realize that all women are naturally promiscuous when the conditions are right (i.e., they're being led by a confident man). You do not need validation and approval from a woman; instead, she needs them from you.

To sum up, as an attractive man, you:

1) Make women come into your reality, not the other way around.
2) Take the lead role, since women are usually passive when it comes to dating and sex.

3) Emotionally arouse women.
4) Are a man of high value, so it is up to women to win your affection.
5) Don't take women too seriously, nor do you take life too seriously.
6) Have your own beliefs, are assertive, and think for yourself.
7) Remember, you don't need her approval!

Almost all of the men I know who are good with women realize these things and place a high value on themselves. Why? Because they (and you) know how to bring women to the highest heights of pleasure!

CHAPTER 11: How to Look Better Than You Ever Thought Possible

How you look is important, but not nearly as much as you think. And not in the ways you probably think. Women don't get judged based on how their men look in the same way that we men get judged on how pretty our girlfriends are.

Look at it this way: imagine you're vacation and you meet a chubby girl in a tropical bar who's just as horny as you are.

You don't have any other prospects for the night, so which would you prefer, having sex with the fat girl, which no one will ever find out about, or masturbating alone in your room?

Most guys would choose the former. This is assuming that she isn't smelly or hideous—just kind of overweight.

Women are the same way. As long as you meet a certain minimum standard—i.e., you aren't morbidly obese or deformed in a ghastly way—you won't be eliminated because of your ugly mug.

Your physical appearance makes up perhaps 20% to 30% of your attractiveness level to women. (Other factors are your level of confidence, how comfortable you are in your skin, how high your status is in society, and how you make women feel in your presence.)

If Johnny Depp—a guy who's a 10 out of 10 in looks (according to my current girlfriend)—were a depressed wimp who slouched all the time and quivered at the thought of speaking to girls he just met, he wouldn't have much success at all.

So, all things being equal, looking good will certainly add to your attractiveness. And in this chapter, you're going to discover the secrets to changing your appearance - as soon as tonight - that will immediately double or triple your looks.

Your shoes

I'll talk about shoes first for a good reason: women notice them a lot more than men do. A lot of guys only have a few pairs of shoes in their closet. Have you seen how many shoes the average woman has? They are highly attuned to what you put on your feet.

So make sure your shoes are nice and stylish and even a bit **bolder** than the plain shoes that the average guy would wear.

When you're at a shoe store, definitely ask women about shoes before you buy! You don't want to make an expensive mistake. Just say, "Hey, I need a quick female opinion. Which shoes do you like, this pair or that one?"

People respond better to a limited number of choices, so I recommend picking out the two pairs that you like the best and then asking for an opinion.

Don't worry, if the woman doesn't like either of them, she will probably check out the store's other shoes on display and let you know what she likes. (Meanwhile, this has gotten you into an extended conversation with a girl, you sly dog!)

At a bare minimum, you'll need four pairs of shoes:
1) Brown casual.
2) Black casual.
3) Brown dressy.
4) Black dressy.

For dressy shoes, I get the kind of shoes that need to be shined. You'll pay a lot for shoes like that (my black dressy shoes cost $150), but they last for years, so they'll be worth the money.

When they're shined up, I get lots of compliments. (I've noticed that women really like shined shoes.)

For casual, I like to wear short boots. I got a really cool pair of brown boots at a flea market for only $20. I get lots of compliments on them from both women and from cool guys.

(Whenever cool people compliment you, that's a sign that you have achieved "cool" social status.)

Boots are also good for shorter guys who want to add a couple inches to their height.

Avoid shoes that make you look like you're trying too hard to fit in, like those $100 name brand tennis shoes with the swoosh on them.

Your hair

If you're like most guys, your hair looks completely awful right now. Maybe you've had the same hairstyle for years, or you try to do the same thing with your hair that your friends do with theirs, even though your hair's different.

It's time for a change. Check out what Hollywood actors and rock stars are doing right now, find a hairstyle you like, and model yours after it. Experiment. As I write this guide, "sex hair" (messed up hair that makes you look like you just got out of a woman's bed) is in.

Consider going to an expensive hairdresser and giving him or her carte blanche to give you a good style for your head shape.

If you really want to look sexy (and you're not homophobic), I recommend going to a gay male hairdresser, since gay guys have an almost supernatural sense of what looks good to women.

And honestly, if your hairline has receded to the point where it's highly noticeable, then shave your head. There's a significant percentage of women who consider a shaved head attractive because baldness radiates masculinity and vigor. If you're an older man, then having a shaved head will make you look years younger.

Comb-overs fool no one, and few women consider horseshoe-shaped hair to be sexually attractive.

Skin

One of the easiest (and free) things you can do to improve your sex appeal to women is to get a tan.

Obviously you don't want to go overboard with it since there's a risk of skin cancer, but sunlight is also necessary for you to get the proper dose of vitamin D, which helps your body produce testosterone. (Also, lack of sunlight has been linked with depressed moods.) In any event, however, get a nice tan and women will think you're sexy.

You can kill two birds with one stone by working out outside.

Shaving

Beards or mustaches are generally out these days, unless you can find a certain look that goes with your features or if you have some deficiencies you need to hide. For example, a goatee or beard can work wonders to obscure a weak chin or acne-scarred cheeks.

Consider shaving your balls and the pubic hair that grows on and around the base of your penis. If you do that, you'll make your penis seem cleaner and more appealing to women. They will give you blowjobs more often.

Just as we prefer women to shave their vulvas (since all that hair gets in the way), women too prefer when we're shaved. An added bonus is that your penis will appear to be longer without all that hair around it.

Don't get squeamish. Shaving your scrotum is much easier than you would think. Try it out with shaving cream and a razor. The hair shaves right off with little trouble.

Shaving your armpits can reduce the amount of bacteria growing under your arms, which reduces foul odors.

Also, make sure you don't have unsightly nose hair or ear hair sticking out. Lots of girls find this to be an instant turnoff. You can find an electric nose hair trimmer at your local discount superstore for less than $20.

Lots of men shave their chests these days, as more women seem to prefer shaved chests to hairy chests. However, that is an individual choice. If you don't care one way or the other, I suggest testing to see what reactions you get when you shave your chest and wear a shirt that exposes it.

If you feel tempted to shave your arms or legs, fight the urge and don't do it. The bottom line is that the vast majority of men who shave these are either a) professional bodybuilders or b) gay.

Dressing

For casual, wear shirts that fit, not shirts that look super baggy. This can be tough, since most clothes you like will not fit. Expect only about 10% of clothes you try on at the store to be suitable.

I can't emphasize enough the importance of not wearing baggy, tent-like clothes that are fashionable only in ghetto high schools or among kids. They will not hide your fat belly.

The best way to obscure your spare tire is to wear shirts that draw attention to your chest, such as shirts with a horizontal stripe across your man-tits.

If you **are** fat, it goes without saying that you should also be hitting the gym (**weightlifting and cardio**) and eating right so that you can slim down.

It also helps with your testosterone levels. Carrying excess body fat (approximately 20% or more above your ideal body weight) can cause your body to have elevated levels of the estrogen hormone. (Ever notice how sometimes really fat guys have "bitch tits"? Now you know why.)

Wear clothes that make you look as close as possible to the ideal male body type, which is tall, with wide shoulders tapering down to a narrow, slender waist. This is a look that women think is hot!

Avoid clothes that make you look different from this ideal body type. For example, fat guys should avoid shirts with horizontal stripes around the waist.

If you're tall and thin, try wearing a jacket or unbuttoned long-sleeve shirt over a tight shirt. Horizontal stripes are good; vertical stripes are bad.

Short guys should avoid horizontal stripes though, since they make them look too wide. Instead, they should think narrow in their clothing choices: narrow shirts and narrow pants.

Stay away from anything too common like pinstripes or the ubiquitous polo shirts that frat boys wear. And no, girls will **not** think you're being original by turning up the collar, since too many guys do that already.

Company logos or sports logos on your shirts? That makes it look like you're trying hard to fit in with the pack. That's good if you want to be a generic guy instead of a loser, but it's more attractive to girls if you stand **above** the pack of guys who are walking billboards.

When dressing casual, you want to give the appearance that you just got dressed after having hot sex with a woman.

So don't tuck in your shirt unless you're wearing a suit. And leave the top two buttons unbuttoned.

Avoid cheesy designs or anything that makes it look like you're **trying too hard** to look cool.

Consider wearing a suit and tie sometimes, especially when you're in situations where other guys dress like slobs, like in college.

Ever notice how women go out of their way to compliment guys wearing suits and ties? A suit and tie are CEO clothes. They communicate status and ambition, and there are no downsides to wearing them.

Of course, you should make sure you're alpha on the inside or you'll come across as a nerd trying hard to make a good impression.

When wearing a suit, have a cotton shirt (plain, not with stripes or anything), cuff links, a dark jacket and pants, and black leather, shined shoes. Wear a nice silk tie, which can even be a bold design. Watch the kind of compliments you get from people. Nothing says authority like a dark suit.

Vintage clothes are in, as long as they're not too flamboyant.

Jeans are also in. Try getting one pair of expensive jeans. Look for slim fit because you want your legs to look slender. Bagginess conveys femininity because it gives you curves like the **female** body ideal.

Matching

I'm continually amazed at how many guys I see making the most obvious mistakes like wearing brown belts with black shoes, so please pay attention to how the colors of your outfit go together.

You need to match all your clothing. You can do this two ways:

> 1) Through similar colors.
> 2) Through colors that contrast significantly.

Colors tend to affect people's mood and energy level, so think about what you want to convey when you get dressed, and then match up the parts of your outfit accordingly.

There are two broad categories—warmth and coolness. Warm colors include yellow, orange, and red. Cool colors include purple, blue, and green.

If you want to do similar colors, have shades of one color, such as light blue jeans and a darker blue shirt.

You can also have colors that are closely related—red and purple, for example, both warm colors that are close to each other on the **color wheel**.

Also dress in colors that are at opposite ends of the color wheel—dark blue jeans with a light brown shirt for instance.

Neutral colors—white and black—go with almost everything. Also consider wearing colors that are mostly white or black—such as beige, which is white tinted with brown—or gray, which is a combination of black and white. But not beige **with** gray.

The color of your accessories (belt, watch, etc.) should match your shoes as closely as possible. Pants should never contrast all that much with your shoes, although your shirt can.

Another rule for clothes that should be obvious but often is not is that they must be clean. Girls are much more attuned to unlaundered or stained clothes than guys are.

How to tell whether clothes need washing:

1) On shirts and pants, look for stains. If you see stains, wash the stains out by rinsing the spot under a water faucet and rubbing it with stain remover. Then toss the article of clothing into the washing machine.

2) Socks and underwear should be worn only once and then washed.

3) Jeans need to be washed when they get stretched out, even if they're not stained.

4) Nothing should smell. If it smells, put it in the laundry.

With wrinkle-free fabric so common today, ironing isn't as necessary as it used to be, except in extreme cases. Some things should always be ironed though, such as oxford shirts (the long-sleeved cotton kind that you wear with a suit).

When wearing a suit, make sure your shirt is lightly starched, or else you'll look sloppy. You don't have to own an iron... just take your stuff to the dry cleaners and let them do it.

Another thing girls appreciate is interesting underwear, since they themselves wear colorful panties. So get something with writing on it or a picture.

The night I met my current girlfriend, she "oohed" and "aahed" over my Spongebob Squarepants boxer shorts. Briefs in dark colors are also an excellent choice.

Accessories

Most guys don't accessorize well, so this is an easy area for you to separate yourself from the pack. The main thing is to make them **subtle yet intriguing**. Avoid coming across as too try-hard.

Look for cool stuff that fits with your personality. A $30 watch with a wide leather band that features unique designs will get you more compliments from women than a silver watch worth thousands since the former displays a lot more originality.

A cool $15 silver vintage ring with an eye-catching pattern will turn 100 times more female eyes than a $500 college graduation ring.

There's wide latitude for accessories, as long as they make you stand out from other guys. Try to avoid things that tons of other guys have, such as armband tattoos and white seashell necklaces. Be unique.

Your Style

There's two kinds of guys—those who get laid and those who don't.

To get laid, find what demographic of people you fit into (e.g., preppies, corporate executives, ghetto boys, college dorm boys), see what the alpha males of that group are wearing, and dress similarly.

In particular, try to be just a little bit cooler than everyone when it comes to your shoes, accessories like your watch or belt, and the way your clothes fit you. (Make sure you look like the male body ideal, with wide shoulders and narrow waist, as described above.)

Don't be *too much* cooler than everyone else or you'll look out of place and weird, or possibly gay. Just be a tad better dressed than the best-dressed guy in the room.

Look around, and it'll become obvious to you what you should wear and what you should avoid. For example, T-shirts with sports logos, beer bottles, or phrases that you wouldn't say in polite company are not attractive to girls and typically are worn only by guys who aren't getting laid that night.

Watch the latest hit movies by popular actors for fashion advice. (As I write this, *Ocean's 12* has some good examples of what's in.)

Also check out TV and magazine ads aimed at the 18 to 35 demographic. By that I don't mean clothing ads (since they tend to wear super expensive clothes), but ads for things like cell phones and airlines. The models in those ads are generally dressed subtly cool in a way that appeals to a wide audience.

When you're shopping for clothes, get opinions from women in the store.

As you come up with your own style that's unique to you, avoid styles that are too common and too plain. I personally like to hit the vintage clothing stores and dress in some of the brighter and tighter early 1980s clothes. That's just me though, as it fits with my personality.

So go for something unique and fashionable that is appropriate for who you are, but don't get too wrapped up in how you look.

Because, while looking good does help, it's not your looks that get you laid, it's your alpha male behaviors and thought patterns.

Women are not just after a good-looking man. They also crave a man with high social status who will give them excitement, passion, and romance. They want a man who will give them a good time and make them feel good.

Along with the style issues, it's important also to develop a strong, masculine body. That means working out and having a good diet.

Not only will hitting the gym make you look healthier, but you will also feel more energetic **and** become more attractive to women because you will have so much more confidence.

The most important thing about how you look, after all is said and done, is that it must be consistent and congruent with who you are. Your clothes create perceptions of you in women. So if you can't back up the perceptions you create, then they will be turned off.

If your clothes say "excitement" the way a Lamborghini's style does, then women will be disappointed if the motor inside is something conventional like a station wagon or SUV.

Your Body

Women used to be able to guess my age before I started exercising six years ago. Sometimes they even guessed older!

Then about six months after I started hitting the gym, women I met were surprised at my age—they thought I was younger.

A few months ago, a hot 26 year-old who took me home with her swore I couldn't be older than 28. (I'm 39.) She genuinely didn't believe me when I told her how old I was.

I used to be fat and flabby; now I'm slender and muscular. On a scale of 1 to 10, my looks used to be about a 4. Whenever I put my picture up on sites such as hotornot.com, I'd routinely get rated around 4 to 5. Today I get rated from 8 to 8.5, and from the compliments that I get from women on my looks, I'd say my hotornot rating is pretty accurate.

You can't do anything about your genetics. Your fitness level, however, is totally within your control, and it is a significant part of what makes you look good to a woman. That's good news for you.

Getting in shape will make you look good in so many ways. Your stomach will flatten and you'll notice your abs becoming more defined. With your muscles growing all over your body, your facial muscles will grow as well, making your skin tighter and less wrinkled.

A Nuts and Bolts Guide to Working Out

The workout I'm going to give you focuses on heavy compound exercises that work many muscles at once and includes some isolation exercises that will hit any muscles that the compound exercises may have missed.

Compound exercises should be the foundation of your workout. Far too many guys in the gym—the ones who just work out before spring break and aren't serious about it—do primarily arm curls and bench press and ignore their legs and back.

This leads to poor posture, and no matter how big your upper body gets, skinny chicken legs don't look good. Women really do look at men's legs.

Heavy compound exercises release tons of testosterone in your body. Besides building muscle, having higher levels of natural testosterone is associated with dominance and sexual power—two traits that are deeply appealing to women.

Monday –
- Three sets of squats.[1] Do 20 reps[2], 15 reps, and then 12 reps.[3]
- Three sets of stiff-legged deadlifts. Do 20 reps, 15 reps, and 12 reps.
- Two sets of calf raises. Do 20 reps, 15 reps, and 12 reps.
- Two sets of arm curls. Do 12 reps and 10 reps.

Tuesday –
- Rest or cardio.

Wednesday –
- Two sets of incline dumbbell presses. Do 12 reps and 10 reps.

---

[1] If you don't know what these exercises are, look them up at http://bodybuilding.com/fun/exercises.htm

[2] Legs and abdominal muscles are made up primarily of slow-twitch muscle fibers, which respond better to higher reps than your upper torso and back.

[3] For each exercise, always use a weight that makes those last 3 -5 reps extremely difficult.

- Two sets of weighted forward-leaning dips.[4] Do 12 reps and 10 reps.
- Two sets of lateral raises. Do 12 reps and 10 reps.
- Two sets of overhead dumbbell presses. Do 12 reps and 10 reps.
- Two sets of weighted sit-ups. Do 20 reps and 15 reps.

Thursday –
- Rest or cardio.

Friday –
- Three sets of deadlifts. Do 12 reps, 10 reps, and 8 reps.
- Two sets of weighted chin-ups. Do 12 reps and 10 reps.
- Two sets of weighted pull-ups. Do 12 reps and 10 reps.
- Two sets of dumbbell rows. Do 12 reps and 10 reps.
- Two sets of bent-over lateral raises. Do 12 reps and 10 reps.

Do a warm-up set or two before you go into your main sets, using about 50% and then 75% of your working weights. For example, if you squat 200 pounds during your main sets, you'd warm up by doing 100 pounds for 8 reps, then 150 pounds for 4 reps.

You should then feel warmed up to go into your work sets. If not, then you should do 2 or 3 more reps

---

[4] If you can't do weighted dips, then do unweighted until you've built up your strength sufficiently.

closer to your work weight. In the example, you would do 175 pounds for 3 reps.

It's important that you go either to failure to near-failure. When I say do 20, 15, and 12 sets, that means do the maximum weight that you can lift that particular number of reps.

Limit your workouts to 50 minutes. Studies have shown that after that point, your muscles are catabolizing (breaking down) too fast.

Give yourself two or three minutes between sets to recover, but remember that you want to be able to do all your exercises within the 50-minute limit.

Immediately after your workout, consume a mixture of protein and carbohydrates. This puts a stop to the catabolic breakdown that you've started by lifting weights and shifts your body towards anabolism (muscle building).

The workout I've outlined is tailored toward muscle growth. If you want to emphasize power, do half the reps.

On Tuesday, Thursday, and Saturday, you should do cardiovascular exercise if you need to lose body fat. I recommend doing high intensity interval training.

High intensity interval training (HIIT) is short but intense, and studies have shown it to be more effective than moderate intensity training. Moderate training consists of activities such as jogging for a half hour, etc.

HIIT is 10 minutes, but it has you alternate between sprinting full speed for one minute and slowly jogging for another minute, then alternating back and forth until the 10 minutes is up.

Although HIIT is much shorter than moderate intensity cardio, you will definitely feel it.

Finally, watch your diet. A popular saying among serious bodybuilders goes, "Muscle is built in the kitchen, not in the gym." To build muscle, your body needs about one gram of protein per pound of bodyweight each day. Good sources are beef, chicken, nuts, tuna, and whey protein powder.

Eat frequent, smaller meals rather than three large meals a day. This ensures that your body has enough protein for protein synthesis within your muscles.

Eat clean, healthy calories. Avoid trans-fats. (Look for "partially hydrogenated" oils and shortening on ingredient labels).

Avoid junk food such as Coke, chips, and white breads. Carbs themselves aren't bad... you just need the right kinds of carbs, like the complex carbohydrates found in oatmeal and whole wheat bread, and fresh veggies and fruit. Avoid starches.

Finally, make sure to drink enough fluids, since your muscles are primarily water.

What it means to look good

Because about 20% to 30% of your attractiveness with girls depends on your looks, when you are more handsome, you'll find that every aspect of your interactions with them will get a boost.

Dressing well, working out, and eating proper nutrition will especially help older guys (30 years old and over). Guys naturally obtain higher status and become more alpha as they age, so if you have a flat stomach as well, it will pay off tremendously.

Not only will you look better, but also when you have nice clothes and a nice body, you will have more self-esteem and feel higher confidence.

Whenever you need an ego boost, you can just look in the mirror. This will help you in so many little ways that build upon themselves and significantly increase the enjoyment you get out of life. So hit the gym, eat right, and wear better clothes.

CHAPTER 12: Important Techniques to Take Control of Your Mindset and Build Your Ideal Personality

I've been telling you lots of valuable secrets, but now it's time for you to take control of yourself. You, not others, are in charge. This means that you need to develop an **internal locus of control** in your life.

Most people have an external locus, meaning that they see forces outside themselves as being in charge of their life. They believe that success is really beyond their control. In a way, this is convenient since it give them someone or something else to blame when things go wrong.

For those with an external locus of control, it doesn't matter how hard they try since life is really a game of luck. If people around them are in a bad mood, then they're in a bad mood.

People with an external locus have trouble with motivation. Usually they don't want to put forth the effort to succeed unless they have already been successful.

They also tend to be afraid of taking risks in life. When they do make mistakes, they assign responsibility to others rather than try to learn from what they did.

As we go through life, we assign explanations for everything. It's deeply embedded within our psyches. Psychologists even have a term for this phenomenon: Attribution Theory.

Studies have shown that successful people tend to have an internal locus. That's because a person with an internal locus believes that **they make their own luck in life**. They believe that the more they strive, the more they will succeed. Anything they want to accomplish is totally within the realm of possibility.

Having an internal locus of control means being **self**-confident and **self**-motivated. It means being optimistic, because you know that your destiny is in your hands.

As you go through your process of self-improvement, you must start attributing internally, as follows:

New way of talking to yourself	Old way of talking to yourself
I did an awesome job.	It was an easy task.
I feel motivated because I choose to.	I feel motivated because a woman just gave me her phone number.
My motivation comes from within, so it's irrelevant that a woman rejected me just now.	I've lost motivation because a woman rejected me just now.
I got an A because I'm smart and studied hard.	I got an A on the test because the teacher was merciful and made it easy.
I've improved myself to the point where I'm so attractive that a lucky woman got to have sex with me tonight. It happened because I created the conditions to make the sex possible.	The stars were aligned just right tonight, so I had sex with a woman on a first date.
I don't litter because I believe it's wrong.	I don't litter because it's against the law.
I know I'm hot because I have a strong psychological reality, I'm in shape, and my spread-out body language conveys how relaxed and in-control I am.	I know I'm hot because I've had sex with so many women.

In life, things work out for me because I make good decisions.	In life, things work out for me because fate is on my side.
I have a successful friendship with a person when both he and I do things for each other.	I have a successful friendship with a person when the chemistry is right.
It is my responsibility to learn.	It is the teacher's responsibility to educate me.
I have high self-esteem. I know I'm capable of accomplishing anything I put my mind to.	I have low self-esteem because I haven't accomplished much in life.
People make money by working intelligently and pursuing their dreams.	Rich people have gotten the right breaks in life.
My life is my hands.	I can't control my destiny.
I feel nervous around women only because I tell myself that I need their approval.	Women make me nervous.

Your attributions affect your behavior. This is the biggest reason why people who attribute things internally are more successful. Self-made millionaires tend to be people who were self-reliant and did what it took to improve their situation.

If you believe you are the kind of man who is attractive to women, then you will find yourself displaying attractive behaviors naturally.

Let's say you chat up a woman in a laundromat. You feel completely outgoing and have a great conversation with her.

After the two of you are finished folding your clothes, you leave with her to get a bite to eat. After a couple hours of conversation, you two head to a bar for a drink. Then you go to her place to get laid.

She found you attractive for many reasons, but most of all it was your high confidence level.

So where does your confidence come from? Does it come from having previously had sex with women? If so, then that's an external attribution.

The problem with external attributions is that they make you vulnerable to a system of rewards and punishments. As long as you get your reward (i.e., sex with women), then your confidence stays high and you stay motivated to keep going to the gym and wearing good clothes.

If you have a string of failures with women, however, your confidence will plummet. Then you quit the gym and just wear whatever.

So it's better to be confident simply because "that's the kind of guy I am" rather than because of anything that happens in the external world.

If you're confident because of your internal attributions, then you'll stay that way no matter how many women don't have the good taste to choose you. (Notice how I didn't say, "no matter how many women reject you"? You gotta think positive!)

By the way, there was a time when I used to be so terrified of speaking to women that my vision blurred, my face turned beet red, and I'd stammer like an idiot. It was all caused by caring what women think.

The permanent solution to this is to **stop thinking that women are important**.

Yes, you read that right.

Thinking that women are important only screws you up when it comes to the game of love. Instead, view them as a source of thrill, excitement, and sex... no more, no less. Don't view every woman as a potential girlfriend, because that causes you to put too much stock in her approval.

Easy Alpha Male Exercise - If you find yourself with an external locus of control, you can help yourself grow out of it by creating a list of targets that you blame for your life not being what it is. Go ahead and make your list right now.

Made your list? Great. Some things you might have on it are:
1) Other people, such as your parents who did a bad job raising you or your boss who holds you back right now. The people in your high school who made fun of you and made you feel bad. These people taught

you to have irrational fear of strangers, so today you feel shy.
2) Your circumstances. You were born into poverty, your uncle hit you, you went to a bad public school and missed out on a lot of the educational opportunities that other people got.
3) Your genetics/God. Your face is asymmetrical, you're short, etc.

I'm not trying to belittle your problems at all. The key is that too often in life we become **immobilized** because of circumstances that are beyond our control. Then we can't effect change.

We can't change the way our parents raised us, so being upset about that today is a waste of time. No matter how upset you get, you can't change what happened.

By looking at your blame list, can you see any real reason why you should be so pessimistic that you do **nothing** to improve your life because of the people on that list? Why give them that power?

Study after study has shown that merely having the belief that we are in control of our situation will have a significant impact on our actions. The more we believe that we are not in control of our situations, the more likely we are to give up.

As you start shifting towards having an internal locus of psychological control, you will become a more positive thinker. You have the power to take action to improve the things that you are currently weak in. If you're ugly for example, then hit the gym, improve your diet, and work on your clothing and grooming.

You will also take responsibility for motivating yourself. You will realize that as you become more determined to improve yourself, and you are persistent with going for the things you want (such as sex), you will increase the chances that you will get them.

The more you believe that you can control your life, the higher your chances of achieving what you want.

Your Thoughts

You're constantly thinking. Most of our feelings come from our thoughts. The good news is that as thinking beings, we have the power to choose our thoughts, and thus our feelings.

We can choose to think (and feel) positively or negatively. The bad news is that it's often easier to think negative thoughts, so we have to **work** to stay positive.

For example, suppose you attend a speed-dating event where every one of the women checks "no" by your name to indicate that they don't want to see you again.

A negative view of this would be to think you're scum, so of course women wouldn't want to talk to you. And what about all those other guys who were much better looking than you? Maybe it would have been a better night if you'd stayed home and played *Halo 2*.

A positive view would be to realize that with every girl, you wrinkled your forehead and leaned forward too far, indicating that you were nervous and trying too hard for approval. Correct those two major body language mistakes, and you'll convey a better impression of yourself next time.

What you think about often becomes a part of your life. If you worry, then you'll find things to worry about. If you're optimistic, then people and good things will be drawn towards you. So if you want to be a successful man, you need to have positive thoughts.

Recalling the past creates a lot of your negative thoughts. Surely you've screwed up before; we all have. The key is to let the past go.

I want to make sure you get this: the past **doesn't exist** anymore, except in your mind. Lay your past mistakes to rest and don't think about them after you've learned lessons from them.

Try to eliminate negative thoughts. Identify sources of negativity in your life and stop allowing them to influence you. Personally, I find negativity in certain individuals, songs, and television shows such as the news. (Don't feel like you have to be a news junkie. If the world comes to an end, someone will tell you!)

Developing a positive mindset

It's all in your mind. That, and your attitude.

"Why would any girl be attracted to me," you think. "I'm too short."

You enter class and sit in your usual spot. The girl who sits in front of you notices you, and then all of a sudden turns around and says, "Can I have a piece of paper?"

"Sure," you say, handing her a sheet.

You say no more to her for the rest of the class. That night, you think back on that girl, dreaming about her as you lie alone in bed, thinking what a loser you are . . .

What you didn't realize was that the girl was making a special effort to talk to you. She didn't really need a piece of paper... she could have just asked another girl for it and not had to worry about the whole male-female dynamic. But she used it as an excuse to talk to you, because she was interested in you. She thinks she sent you an obvious signal.

But you had no idea.

For something to happen to you, you have to believe in it first. In our example, if you'd believe you are an attractive man, then you'll be receptive to girls coming into your life. But if you don't believe it's a possibility, then you will psychologically block it out, even when it's blatant like the girl who asked for paper.

Expect good things to happen to you. That way you'll seize opportunities.

Identify negative thoughts when they crop up and let them go. As you eliminate negative thoughts, let positive thoughts and feelings flow. Choose to be confident and happy on the inside, no matter what happens to you on the outside.

Be pleased with yourself and realize that you will be happy no matter what happens. Your confidence comes from within, and you improve yourself everyday because that's fundamental to who you are.

Here are a few ways to develop a more positive mindset:

1) **Constantly see yourself as the person you would like to be.** Imagine how you would behave and what sorts of happiness you would harvest from your life if you were that ideal person. Visualize the amount of money you would make, the house you would live in, and the physique you would have. Avoid negative influences in your life such as friends who make pessimistic comments.
2) **As you recall the past, think only about your successes.** Recognize that any failures you had are only

temporary and more the result of bad luck than any problem fundamental to you.

3) **Assume success** (though don't be attached to it). View yourself as relaxed, and expect that because you are the dream lover of every woman, of course you will eventually find the success that you want. Smile as you enjoy what it feels like to be a man who's attractive to women.

4) Start identifying the thoughts that you have. Remember that your thoughts are under your control, so you can have whatever visualization you desire. Because your reality is what you believe, **use your visualizations to pump yourself up** rather than shoot yourself down. As Albert Einstein said, "Your imagination is your preview of life's coming attractions."

5) **Do affirmations**, which I will explain next.

Changing the way you talk to yourself through affirmations

I've had a lot of success in changing my attitudes, and much of it has come from saying affirmations. Affirmations are statements that you repeat over and over again until you believe them.

As you go throughout your day, you are constantly making statements to yourself. Often these are **bad** affirmations, such as:

"I'm such a loser."
"I'm not good at talking to random women."
"I'm depressed."
"I'm in a bad mood."
"I'm lazy."
"I'm stuck in a dead end job and can't do anything about it."
"Life sucks."

Ouch! I really can't type any more examples, because it's conjuring up old painful memories of how I used to think! But you get the idea, and perhaps if you took the time, you could come up with a long list of negative beliefs that you hold.

The problem with negative thoughts is that they have a reinforcing effect. The more you think them, the more you back them with feeling, the more they become ingrained in your mind.

The more you repeat a statement to yourself, along with **visualizing** it and **feeling** it, the more you start to actually believe it. Too much negative self-talk, and your problems and insecurities pile up.

The good news, however, is that you can start making **positive** affirmations. By repeating new beliefs over and over again to yourself, you can program them into your mind.

Take the affirmation, "I am becoming more extroverted." At first your mind will raise its BS meter and try to block it because it's such a radically new idea. After all, you have spent years and years telling yourself that you're unsociable.

Then one day, after a few weeks of doing your affirmations several times a day, you do something that you **never** would have done a month before—maybe you are waiting to check out at the grocery store and automatically decide to make light banter with the other people in line. You do it without even thinking, because it's becoming part of your new personality. It's a truly amazing feeling when it happens.

So recognize that affirmations work gradually. They're so slow that it's tough to see them having an effect. Just keep plowing through, keep saying them, and before too long you'll notice yourself behaving in new ways.

Affirmations can do three things:

1. Change a belief about yourself, which adjusts your personality accordingly.

For example, if you use the affirmation, "I am becoming a positive thinker," it will make you more optimistic. You'll start to have thoughts like "that wasn't so bad" and "let's look on the bright side."

2. Reinforce a belief about yourself.

I've always been happy with the way my hair looks. So if I affirm, "I have awesome hair," it helps me become the kind of person with inner confidence who always sees the glass as half full.

3. Motivate yourself.

You could use the affirmation, "I talk with women whom I find attractive." Then your mind will focus on ways you can chat up such women.

You'll have thoughts such as, "I really need to go to the mall to see if I can find some women" or "I wonder when the next speed dating event is." At the grocery store when you see a pretty woman you'll think of any excuse to talk with her like "Excuse me, do you know which avocados are ripe?"

Affirmations work because you become what you think about. They force your mind into a certain manner of thinking, and when you use the affirmations long enough, those new thoughts become your new reality.

You should not just **say** the words of your affirmations to yourself, but you should **feel** what the words are saying and **visualize** the new reality. That way you experience the affirmation using your three major senses (sight, hearing, and feeling).

For example, one of my affirmations I think to myself when I'm walking down the street is, "I enjoy being a completely confident alpha male." When I say it, I feel myself relax my muscles and move more slowly, with my head held high. I visualize my ideal self and become happier.

When you're by yourself at home or in your car, say your affirmations out loud. You fully engage your hearing when you say them out loud. Of course, you should also engage your sight by vividly imagining them, and your feelings, when you have the surge of emotion throughout your body as you imagine your affirmations to be true.

When you first start programming yourself for a new trait, phrase the affirmation in the present progressive verb tense. By this I mean instead of saying, "I feel happy with my life," it's better to say, "I **am feeling** happier with my life as time goes on."

This overcomes a lot of the resistance that you may put up to your new affirmation. Though you say, "I feel happy with my life," you think, "No I am **not** a happy person." Using the present progressive tense overcomes that.

Once you feel as if you are much happier than you used to be, then you can switch toward affirming it is true: "I feel completely happy." As you keep saying your affirmation, your personality will reflect it ever increasingly until it has been virtually fully ingrained in the new you.

From time to time, you'll need to review and repeat your old affirmations. This prevents you from sliding back into your old mindsets.

Affirmations are sort of like weightlifting for your mind. Just as you need to keep pumping iron to keep the physique that you want, so too do you need to maintain your new thoughts to keep your ideal personality.

When you develop your affirmations, use the technique that works the best for you. Some people are more auditory-oriented, so they benefit from recording their affirmations and then playing them back in a continuous loop.

If you're on a Windows PC, the best way to do this is create your own audio files on your computer using a microphone and the Sound Recorder program that comes pre-installed on most Windows systems.

Others tend to be more visually oriented and should visualize their affirmations as they say them to themselves. I am kinesthetically oriented (motivated primarily by physical sensations), so people like me should try to feel their affirmations as if they were true.

Even though you may have your main way to do affirmations, try to hit all your senses. An additional method that helps everybody is to write affirmations down on paper.

When you do the first few sentences, your mind will be full of doubt, but as you move down the paper, it's almost miraculous how much your mind will change to adopt the new belief you're affirming.

Easy Alpha Male Exercise – It's time to make your own affirmations. As you formulate them, here are some rules that will help you:

1) Affirm traits, beliefs and **realistic** accomplishments that you want to motivate yourself to have. (If you

affirm "I have 10,000 girlfriends," then you set yourself up for disappointment, since that's physically impossible. Five or ten is better.)

2) Make your affirmations as strong as possible. "I am completely confident" is better than "I am confident."

3) Try to phrase each affirmation in no more than a dozen or so words.

4) The mind responds better if you make positive statements. "I feel totally relaxed in social situations" is preferable to "I don't feel nervous in social situations."

5) When you want to GIVE UP a trait, use the phrase "release the need," e.g., "I release the need to feel threatened by other guys."

Some affirmations that have worked well for me are:

- I am comfortable and confident.[5]

- I have super high self-esteem.

- I am an alpha male.

- I enjoy making light conversations with girls.

- I am the dream lover of every woman.

- I think optimistically.

- I feel secure in myself.

---

[5] Remember, if you are not at all comfortable and confident, phrase it "I AM BECOMING comfortable and confident."

- I release the need to care what women think.
- I move through life with elegance, dignity, and style.
- I am pleased with myself.
- I feel relaxed, calm, and in control.
- I move my hands and head slowly, because I am alpha.
- I relax my body and spread out.
- I feel highly sexual with women.
- I love myself.
- I am good in bed.
- I am an amazing, ultra-confident guy.
- My life is fun.
- I feel comfortable talking with other people.
- I take up space wherever I am, because I radiate confidence.
- I feel calm when I enter people's personal space.
- I touch people when I talk with them.
- My facial muscles are relaxed.

- I have high standards, so I am a challenge for girls.
- I am interesting.
- I am unpredictable.
- I'm like a god.
- I am good-looking.
- I am an attractive man.
- I build trust with anyone I talk to.
- I am tough and powerful, like a champion boxer.
- I am so incredibly attractive and skilled in bed that women become dripping wet around me!
- With women, I persist towards either sex or rejection.
- I enjoy rejection, because it means I went for it.
- I am adventurous.
- I release the need for other people's approval.
- I am a winner.
- I am assertive.
- When it comes to sex, I'm a devilish bad boy.

- I am a good catch for any woman.
- I am the dream lover for every woman.
- I focus on positive emotions.
- I am fun and interesting.
- I am sexual.
- I'm completely satisfied and totally relaxed.

Self-Hypnosis

Self-hypnosis is a terrific tool that you can use to program your mind. It operates on the principle that when you relax yourself and stop thinking, your brain becomes acutely receptive to suggestions. These suggestions then take root in your mind and make their mark in your life.

Your brain is a very complex organ. It's constantly thinking, rationalizing, and reasoning. Often you put up resistance to taking on new thoughts and attitudes that you need to create a better life for yourself.

Like affirmations, self-hypnosis is a gradual process. Each time you do it, you'll program your mind toward what you want, but that programming usually fades. So you need to repeat your self-hypnosis sessions from time to time until your mind becomes fully convinced of the new ideas you are acquiring.

You don't need any fancy equipment or software for this. Simply use a cassette recorder. To effectively create and use your self-hypnosis tape, follow these instructions.

- Make sure there are no distractions. Turn your cell phone off and unplug your land line. You don't want to record for 20 minutes and have it be interrupted!
- Don't worry about stumbling over words while you're reading the script. Just keep plowing through. When you listen to the tape later, any speaking errors that you made will seem so trivial that you'll hardly bother noticing them.
- Make sure there's no background noise such as air conditioners or road traffic.
- When you start reading the script, use your regular speaking voice. Speak with a moderate pace—not too high-energy nor too slow. Then as the recording moves into the talk about the "relaxing oxygen," slow it down and use a more relaxed voice. When you listen to the tape, you're going to be moving into a deeply tranquil state, so you need the tape to have a calm voice on it.
- When listening to the tape, again turn off any phones or other potential distractions. You don't want to be deep in repose only to have it get violently interrupted.

- Get comfortable, with your body spread out and relaxed, when you listen to your tape. I like to lie down on a couch.
- Listen with an open mind. Follow the instructions you have given yourself.

Tape Script

Close your eyes. Take a deep breath. Allow yourself to feel relaxed.

I want you to feel all your tensions from today, all your stress-inducing worries, gathered in a tight little ball right at your forehead. Feel the tension of how you've worried about rejections from girls in the past.

Feel the tensions from work, your career, your ambitions, and everything else gathering up in your forehead.

Now I want you to imagine all those tensions draining away. Let them drain out of your forehead and down your face, down your chin and neck, down your chest, your stomach, waist, and then down your legs and through your toes until they leave your body.

All your tension is leaving your body as you relax more and more.

As you breathe in, I want you to imagine that you're breathing in air that is warm and relaxes you. Feel the relaxing oxygen give you a warm, tingly feeling all through your chest cavity. Feel the relaxation radiate out of your chest and then throughout your body.

Allow your breathing to become deeper, bringing in more and more of the relaxing oxygen. With every breath, you fall deeper and deeper into relaxation.

[Pause 15 seconds.]

As you feel completely relaxed and focus totally on my voice, I want you to repeat these affirmations to yourself mentally as I say them.

- I feel great about myself. [After each of these, pause to allow the listener—i.e., you—to repeat them.]

- Being an optimist allows me to achieve anything I want in life.

- I am constantly becoming better.

- There is no limit to what I can accomplish, so I will program my mind to become fabulously successful beyond my wildest dreams.

- I know this will work because I am adopting the same mindset as men who are already successful.

Now that you have said your affirmations, I will count to ten, and with each number I count out, you will become even more relaxed. One, more relaxed. Two. Three. Four, deeper into relaxation. Five. Six. Seven. More relaxed. Eight. Nice. Ten.

You are now at the deepest level of relaxation you can be in while still being awake. You will now use this opportunity to program your mind for your maximum benefit.

You're a sexy guy. You can make a woman just as happy as any other guy can.

You desire sex with hot women.

You're in control of your own life. Nobody else is. You can choose to become completely successful in whatever you do, and you enjoy having that power.

Because you have such a powerful, positive state, you radiate an aura of poise, brilliance, and quiet, steady confidence.

You've got an awesome mind, and your willpower is becoming stronger and stronger. You are determined to reach your goals.

Now take another breath, and continue to enjoy the feeling of deep relaxation. Say the following affirmations to yourself with me.

- I release the need to allow other people to control my life. [*Again, pause after all these to let your listener—i.e., you— repeat them!*]

- I only need approval from myself.

- I couldn't care less what other people think of me, because I'm the one who's in charge of my life.

- I am a dynamite alpha male. I walk like I'm a badass, and I think incredibly highly of myself.

- I love women because they are a source of fun and pleasure in my life.

- When I have sex with a woman, I do so enthusiastically and for the total satisfaction of myself and my beautiful partner.

- I lust after sex with women. I love to make love.

- I love to give love.

Now it's time for you to just listen and not feel the need to repeat anything. Continue to enjoy the way you feel so relaxed. Just let your mind be totally at ease as you let these thoughts flow in.

When you're with a woman, you stay calm and relaxed, no matter what happens, because you are in control of your life. You don't put all that much concern in what she thinks of you, because you know that you're a fun, interesting guy and she's fortunate just to be with you.

You are the most important person in the world. You are completely awesome, and any woman would be lucky to have you. You deserve everything you get, because you radiate warmth and happiness.

Never again will you be a subservient to anyone. Not to any person—male or female.

You are a natural leader, not a follower.

You live an active life. You have fun and find thrills everyday, even in little things.

You take care of your health because you want to be strong and attractive and live a long time.

Your life is interesting. You enjoy telling women stories about the fascinating things that happen in your life.

You feel an intense desire to achieve financial success. You know that you can accomplish anything you dream of, and you enjoy pushing yourself toward that dream.

You feel ambitious and you want to have success with women, with your health, with good friends, with financial wealth, and with the hobbies and passions that you enjoy.

Now take a deep breath and relax.

Pause for a moment, and enjoy the feeling of being totally in control of your life. You can be completely successful if you choose to, and you'll love every minute of that success. You love when your dreams come true, as they already are.

Soon you'll come out of your state of relaxation and become more awake. As I count to five, become more and more awake. One. Two, more awake. Three.

As you awaken, you feel totally refreshed, full of energy and vigor, and massively confident. Four, open your eyes. You're an alpha male. Five, fully awake. You feel totally refreshed and in a great mood!

CHAPTER 13: Severing Your Attachment to Outcomes

She: "So what do you do for a living?"
You (thinking, "Gee, I wonder what I should tell her. If she likes my answer, I'll get laid. If not, I'll have to masturbate!"): "Umm, I am an, um, engineer."
She (getting bored): "Oh, OK. Yeah, that's cool. Hey I need to go call my friend."

When you talk to a woman, be relaxed. To do this, focus on right now and pay attention to what's going on outside of you instead of analyzing and second-guessing yourself.

When you think too much, it interferes with your mind's ability to socially vibe. So when you're talking with a woman, don't analyze or judge yourself. Be fluid rather than systematic.

Focus on the here and now. Don't be concerned with the results; they'll take care of themselves.

In the example above, rather than doing all that thinking about what will happen later, focus on what the girl is saying. Be relaxed and tell her the story about how you always wanted to invent new things as you were growing up, and now as an engineer you can fulfill your dreams.

And don't forget to let yourself have fun, too. Relax and don't attach much importance to any of your conversation or behavior.

Remember: you're not attached to an outcome. You have no expectations.

All you're going to do is create the right conditions for a lay to take place, and then go with whatever happens. If it happens, great. If not, just shrug. There'll be other opportunities.

In life there are some things you cannot control, and other things you can. The key to happiness is to focus on the things that you can control while not attaching too much importance to the things you can't. So relax and enjoy yourself.

One of the winningest college basketball coaches of all time was John Wooden of UCLA. If UCLA lost a game, Wooden taught his players to view it as not being a big deal. UCLA was on its way to winning, but the clock ran out before it could.

I want you to view women the same way. When it comes to women, you're going to get laid eventually, I promise. If you display attractive qualities and persist with enough women, you will always have sex... if you are given enough time.

An example of something you don't have an attachment to the outcome of would be surfing the web. You do it because it's fun, not because you need to do it and stress out about it. You don't expect anything in particular.

With women too, you should not be dependent on any outcomes. If you feel like you NEED to get laid, it will drain your energy and make you feel negative every time you have a failure with a woman.

Instead, just surf her!

Believe me, women have a keen sense for when a man has an agenda. If you have a specific **goal** of getting laid, you will give off vibes of neediness. This makes you look lame.

So forget about what might or might not happen at the end of the date. What the two of you are doing right now should be fun and enjoyable for both of you. If she thinks you'll demand sexual servicing at the end, then she'll think you're pushy.

When you have no expectations, you will be a lot more laid back.

If you have any goal, it should be "increasing the likelihood of getting laid." You'll do this by creating the conditions under which sex with a woman can take place, then nudging the interaction towards the lay.

It's completely natural to talk to a woman even if she's a complete stranger. Be sexual but non-threatening and completely patient. You don't want her to detect that you have any expectations.

Keep your interaction natural and let it flow. Human biology will take its course.

CHAPTER 14: Getting Over Your Insecurities

Ever say these things to yourself?

- *"I'm too pimply-faced."*

- *"I'm too fat."*

- *"I'm too poor."*

- *"I live with my parents."*

- *"I don't have a car."*

- *"I'm so painfully shy!"*

I want you to think about any internal beliefs that you hold which are preventing you from believing that you are attractive to women.

Because your reality is whatever you create, you need to destroy the bad internal beliefs that are making you unconfident and unattractive to women.

I'm not going to claim this is easy, because it isn't. I used to be painfully shy. Although my real problem was my fear of talking to people (especially girls), I rationalized it by telling myself things like, "I value privacy and want everyone to stay out of my business."

It wasn't until I dropped my ego and took a realistic assessment of my life that I realized shyness was a core problem for me. This required me to find my deep-rooted beliefs. I realized that I put too much concern in what other people thought of me. The thought of getting rejected made me afraid.

Once I'd identified the true core belief that was holding me back, I was able to drop my ego and confront that belief head on. For me that was an amazing breakthrough, because once I'd dropped my ego, I permanently got over my shyness around women. It literally happened overnight.

So from that point onward, whenever I talked to people, I worked on focusing externally—i.e., on them and on what the conversation was about—not on internal things such as, "I want this person to like me."

Conversely you may have certain internal beliefs that serve you well. Identify these also and reinforce them. I happen to be genetically gifted when it comes to building muscle. So as I think of myself as a muscular man, it helps my confidence level.

Easy Alpha Male Exercises -
1) Identify the good core beliefs about yourself that you hold.
2) Reinforce them by amplifying what's good about you.
3) Identify your bad core beliefs. Eliminate those.

Granted, this won't happen instantly unless you fully open your mind to it and put out full effort to do those three exercises.

Even if you're skeptical, if you work on it slowly but surely it **will** happen. Take baby steps to observe your behaviors and thoughts, and isolate those thought patterns which are good, and those which you want to change.

And do yourself a favor and save all your analyzing for **later**, when you're at home by yourself, not when you're with a woman.

When you're with a woman, keep yourself focused outwardly and just think about the conversation at hand. This will cause you to feel relaxed and therefore more attractive to her because you're projecting confidence, which increases your likelihood of getting laid.

CHAPTER 15: Handling Your Fears of Rejection

Picture it: you're about to try to talk to a hot girl. You see her standing there in the magazine section of the supermarket, occupying herself with Cosmo.

Her blonde hair is silky and smooth. Her skin is clear and radiant. Her waist is slender. And wow, look at the nice shape of those tits!

You feel the tension.

Excuses pop into your head: "I'm really in a tired mood"; "I didn't dress that well"; "I don't know what to say to her;" "I don't have condoms with me."

The negative self-talk in your head makes you decide not to approach. Your chances of having sex with her now go to absolute zero. You get your groceries, go home, and sleep by yourself that night. You've just shot yourself down—the girl didn't do a thing.

You didn't hesitate because you were truly tired, or badly dressed, or the words wouldn't come (and you can always buy condoms on the way to a lay).

Your real problem was fear. You didn't make the approach because you were afraid of rejection. "I wish I could hurry up and get over this anxiety about chatting up women I don't know," you tell yourself.

"Once I do get over it, then I'll approach them like mad."

The trouble with this sort of thinking is that it programs you for failure. The truth is that **we always feel afraid when we enter a new, unfamiliar situation**. It's a psychological reality of human beings.

The only way to get rid of the fear is to do what you need to do—i.e., approach women—despite the fear. You have to push through. If you've ever done this in sports, it's just like that.

I used to be so afraid of talking to girls that my vision blurred. I kept making these excuses that I would only approach women when my fears went away. I kept waiting. And waiting.

My fears never went away. I was immobilized, unable to figure out why I was so scared to talk to women, and wasted many days and nights refusing to do so until I could feel okay rather than frightened.

Truth is, virtually all men have anxiety when it comes to talking to women, because, let's face it, rejection sucks. It's like a body blow to your ego.

Everyone has an inner sense of self (i.e., self-esteem), which they desire to keep at a high level. Ideally, your self-worth will come from within, and you won't have to depend on others for it.

When this happens, it will become irrelevant what any woman thinks of you. If she likes you, that's great; if not, then so what? You can't control what she thinks.

Don't let a woman's opinion of you matter too much. **Everyone** feels fear at an unfamiliar situation. It is normal and natural. The fear only goes away when the situation becomes familiar.

If you don't push through the fear, you'll be extremely vulnerable and paranoid. Sure, you can back off and not approach, and then you'll never get rejected. But then you'll be alone, always a sad loser who never got laid.

Here's the bottom line: everyone has an imaginary companion who'll be with you your entire life. His name is Fear.

If you allow this companion to take control of your life, then he'll put you in a straightjacket.

But Fear can also be your loyal companion. When you hop on the wild roller coaster of life, engaging in an infinite number of exhilarating undertakings, Fear will come along with you.

He won't get in your way, but he'll always be there as long as you're doing new things. When you feel fear, it's a sign that you're doing something new and exciting.

How To Eliminate Your Fear

To eliminate your fears about chatting with women, you need to do three things:

1. **Have no expectations.** Be social for the sake of being social. Nothing else.
2. **Chat with women.** Remember that the only way to get over your fear is by doing the thing you fear. The more you do it, the easier to gets, because your attitude about any sort of negative experiences like rejection will become, "Been there, done that, it's no big deal."
3. **Identify your thoughts that make you nervous.** Then eliminate them.

Because fear is normal, all guys feel anxiety when it comes to chatting up women when they're not used to it. So as I said, don't feel like your fears are unusual. Instead they mean you're **going for it**.

Now, what separates guys like you from the rest of the guys out there is **what you do about your fear**.

Most men let fear paralyze them… and not just about chicks, but about other things in life like their careers… which is why, unfortunately, most guys will never find the success that they desire.[6]

The reason most men never confront their fears is because they fail to look at where it comes

---

[6] I want to again commend you for getting this book. Taking that step to improve yourself will automatically reap rewards for you far and away above what you otherwise would have achieved.

from. It comes… from inside of you. The problem is with you, not with the women who reject you.

So the next time you talk with women you've just met, do so without any expectations. Have no goals.

I'm inclined to be an introvert, as I discuss previously. To overcome my shyness, I would force myself to chat up **everybody**, no matter who they were.

I'd talk with hot girls, ugly girls, fat girls, old people, men, children, and families walking dogs. It didn't matter who. I'd talk with them about neutral topics having nothing to do with picking up women.

The net result from all of that was I became really good at chatting up anybody. I no longer felt afraid, because I'd kept doing the thing I feared until it no longer frightened me.

After that, however, I made a mistake. I said to myself, "Since I'm so good at talking to people and have become an outgoing person, why am I wasting time in conversation with anyone other than hot chicks?"

After all, as an alpha male, I thought, I was a man of high value and had time only for women who were beautiful.

So I limited the people I talked to… and my anxiety about talking to random women swept over me once again. It was as if I'd never had all that practice chatting up strangers in the first place.

At that point I realized it was because I was **outcome-dependent**. Because I had thoughts in my mind about having sex with the woman *before I'd even opened my mouth to say "hi,"* I would crash and burn. It sucked.

So at this point, here's something I want you to try. Whenever you go out, talk to two people, (or two groups of people), but do it just for practice. Don't do it for real. Don't try to pick up any girls from those conversations.

Because it's just for practice, don't limit yourself to just talking to hot women. In fact, if you're looking for easy conversations, I've found that elderly people (both males and females) and fat women are easiest to talk to. Perhaps it's because people in those demographic groups tend to be the loneliest.

If it helps, set up a time limit for your practice interactions, like that you'll talk to one person for 30 seconds and then bail out of the conversation. (Say something like, "Well, I'm on my way to meeting a friend. Pleasure chatting with you." And then walk away without making a big deal out of it.)

Once you've done your practices and feel warmed up, you can chat up hot chicks. Again though, although it's best if you feel horny, don't think about sex-related outcomes.

For example, if a chick passes by you in a hallway, just say, as if the thought had just occurred to you, "Hey. I need quick female opinion on something."

Then ask her something you genuinely want a woman's opinion on.

Besides having practice conversations, another trick a fried of mine taught me was to think of something funny before you chat up a stranger. Tell yourself a joke and then laugh. That'll put you in a good mood when you talk to the person.

Finally, you reach a point that you've chatted up so many women that negative responses on their part don't phase you one bit. You'll have an attitude like, "Ha, how original... I've had tons of women give me that exact same 'clever' rude comment."

As Tyler Durden put it in the movie *Fight Club*, "Let the chips fall where they may." Stop trying to control your outcome with chicks.

If you have no outcome in mind, you won't care if the chick acts like a bitch.

Now I just look back on the rejections I've gotten and laugh. I've chatted up women so much that rejection usually bores me, but amuses me when it's done in a novel way. Success with women comes from not putting any pressure on yourself.

To get a bit more psychological, there's really no such thing as "being nervous," like it's something genetic. There's no such thing as the "fear bug" or "nervousness flu" invading your body.

All feelings of nervousness come from within. You have a certain series of thought processes that you go through, at the end of which you wind up feeling whatever emotion your thoughts lead you to.

Recently, I coached one guy, James, who said to me, "I would reject myself if I were a girl!"

Now, with thoughts like that, it's no wonder he didn't have much success with women! He was setting himself up for failure.

It worked like this:

1. James pictured chicks rejecting him.

2. James felt tense in his body, rather than relaxed and sexual.[7]

3. James over-thought the whole process, preventing him from having free flowing conversations.

Perhaps it's been similar for you when you feel nervous around women? Don't feel bad. Tons of guys—even guys you'd consider to be "ladies men"—have been there at one time or another. You'll get over it. As they did.

What you can do to break your nervousness is to, again, identify your negative thoughts. And then change them.

---

[7] Look at it this way. If you don't feel relaxed and sexual, how do you expect the woman to feel that way?! You as the alpha male must take the lead. That means you must feel relaxed and sexual, so that the woman will follow.

Instead of thinking, "Oh my God, this chick is going to act like a bitch to me because I fumble my words"... think, "It's awesome that I'm talking to this girl I just saw in the store, because even she rejects me, that means I've gotten her out of the way, and I'm one step closer to finding my dream girl."

When you're nervous, notice the areas in your body where you feel tense, and then let your muscles relax in those areas. That will automatically cause you to feel less tense, because on a neurological level, nervousness often follows muscle tension (rather than the other way around like one would think).

For me, I feel tension in my face and jaw when I'm nervous. So when I relax my jaw and facial muscles, it tells my mind that it's time to feel relaxed rather than nervous.

Finally, there's one more way to reduce anxiety that involves a visualization exercise. Before you even open your mouth to say something to a woman, visualize the situation as if it has already occurred and she has just rejected you.

That way, you'll feel happy about it because...

- At least you **went for it,** as an alpha male who goes through life making no apologies for his desires.

- Each rejection means you're one step closer to success.

- Each rejection makes your conversational ability that much better, since you've been further desensitized to the whole process.

So concentrate on how you'll feel afterwards, and talk to the woman as if the rejection has already occurred (and you feel happy for it), rather than making yourself nervous before you've even opened your mouth.

Ignore The Dating Advice Books!

"You never know, your fears of rejection may be unfounded. She may be dying for you to make your approach."

That's the sort of advice you find in the "Dating for Idiots" guides you find in the bookstores. Ignore it —it's for beta males.

Such advice is based on the assumption that rejection is something you should fear. Instead look at it as something to celebrate. Why, you ask? Because it means you made your approach and went for it!

Think about it: if you went away for a year and came back to find out your favorite college basketball team made the NCAA Final Two, then lost, would you feel let down, or proud they'd had the guts to go for it and make it that far? That's what I mean!

And have no illusions about this – unlike what the "Dating for Idiots" books say, you **will** get rejected, and it will happen a **lot**.

View your interactions with women with the 80/20 rule that businessmen use—i.e., just as 80% of your profits come from 20% of your customers, 80% of your pleasure will come from 20% of the chicks you interact with.

The most profitable businesses are those that focus on the top 20% of customers. They're more than happy to forget about the unprofitable 80% and let those people go to their competitors.

It should be the same thing with women. Don't even think about the ones you can't derive pleasure from. Let the other guys worry about them.

But What if a Woman Does Reject You, and it Really Hurts… Bad?

No matter how bad you get rejected, do not allow it to phase your reality. There's no reason to feel bad. Remember, your manly desires are totally natural and normal. An alpha male never feels ashamed for his high sex drive. Instead, if anything, he feels **proud** for having gone for it.

I know sometimes rejections can be painful. I've had **evil** rejections by women before. One chick screamed, "Go away!" at me before I could even get out my initial sentence.

Another time a woman got some guy to try to start a fight with me just because I tried to talk with her. I managed to get away without coming to blows with the dude, but I felt like a total chump afterwards.

There's nothing you can do about rejection. If you're out in the field chatting with women, they **will** happen. But almost all of the time, as I've explained, they're something to **celebrat**e.

But in those cases where the rejection is so hideous it burns a hole in your heart, the best thing to do is to allow the memory of the rejection to vanish.

That's what I do, and it's worked for me. In fact, I've probably been rejected worse than the two examples I gave, but the memories of those are quite literally gone from my mind. I'll explain how you can do this exercise yourself.

I learned this memory-vanish exercise from Tony Robbins, and it's based on the mental visualization principles from Neuro Linguistic Programming, a form of hypnosis. Here's what you do.

1. Make a picture in your mind of the horrible rejection.
2. Make that picture as big as possible and bring it close to you. Feel the burn of the rejection. Make it intense.
3. Now start moving the picture away from you.
4. As it's moving away from you, make it black and white.

5. Keep moving it, until it's so far away that it's just a tiny speck.
6. Now watch the tiny black and white image start pulsating to circus music.
7. As the tiny, far-away image moves in rhythm with the carnival tunes, have it now move so far away that it burns up in the sun.

No longer is the memory such a big deal, is it?

CHAPTER 16: Why Improve Yourself?

Making a determined effort to improve yourself can have enduring benefits no matter what the final outcome. Consider my own example: I still am more introverted sometimes than I'd like to be, yet on the whole, I have far greater social skills than I used to. I'm not 100% where I want to be yet, but I'm still a helluva lot better than I was.

So remember this: **even if you make great strides overall, yet fall short, you will still be a better and happier man than if you had never attempted anything at all.**

CHAPTER 17: Using the Body Language of an Alpha Male

Watch a man with high status--Brad Pitt, George Clooney, or the CEO where you work--and you'll notice that they move differently than the rest of us. They give off vibes that they are hot stuff, and because of that, women get soaking wet over them.

You, too, can create that aura that makes you attractive to women.

Have you ever noticed the way your friends look when they feel like shit? They're looking down at the ground with their arms crossed, slouching, and giving off other non-alpha behaviors.

Now, think about successful guys. They've got girls all over them and some great body language going on.

Here are some body language pointers (and by the way, if you think they're easy, you're right... you can make these changes as early as **tonight** and have even the hottest girls clamoring for your attention):

1) **Relax.** This is the most important mental state for you to be in.

a) Don't allow yourself to feel worried.

Just let your worries go, since you can't solve any problem by worrying. So suck it up, and quit thinking about what *might* go wrong. Just live life.

Now, I know what I just said is easier said than done (to use an old—but relevant in this case—cliché). You've spent your whole life up until now dwelling on thoughts that make you feel worried.

But what is this emotion we call "worry"? When you think about it, it's simply the fear of what might happen in the future. Essentially you're punishing yourself by feeling upset **before** anything bad has happened. It makes no logical sense to worry!

So the solution is to avoid contemplating your worrisome thoughts anymore. Identify them for what they are—toxic to your emotional state—and let them go.

Simply not dwelling on negative outcomes that make you feel upset will reduce 90% of your worries.

b) Breathe through your abdomen rather than your chest.

When you breathe, imagine that you're bringing air down to your stomach. Feel your belly rise and fall as you breathe.

c) Avoid nonverbal behaviors that are the opposite of relaxation:

- Raising your shoulders.
- Wrinkling your forehead.
- Fidgeting with your hands and/or legs.
- Tightening your facial muscles.

d) Relax all your muscles and slow down all of your movements a notch.

Alpha males generally move unhurriedly, as if they are in control of time itself. Beta males are nervous and make jerky movements. Imagine you are standing and walking through a swimming pool, where your movements are slow and fluid.

e) Relax your eyes and eyelids.

Beta males hold their eyelids wide open because they are so nervous. Their eyes dart all around. Instead let your eyelids rest. Look straight ahead. Only give things your attention if they interest you. While you're out and about, do the affirmation to yourself, "I am sexual, I am relaxed, and I am in control."

f) If someone wants your attention, move your head slowly.

A trait common to many beta males is being so eager to please that when someone calls their name, you see them spin their heads toward the person unnaturally fast.

2) Feel masculine and powerful.

Visualize that you are a masculine man. Do things in your life that make you feel manly, like lifting weights and working out with a punching bag. Take care of your health.

3) Realize that you are a man of high value.

Focus on your qualities and ignore your deficiencies. To become completely confident, think thoughts such as, "I am the shit."

Sound arrogant? Look at it as therapy to get over your lack of confidence. Obviously you'll want to moderate at some point once you become successful and **know** you're awesome (so that you don't act like a prick), but until then think constantly about your greatness.

Treat people as if they are already in awe of you before they even met you. If you have to, visualize Elvis Presley: "Thank yuh, thank yuh verra much…"

4) Feel comfortable in your own skin.

An alpha male is happy with or without any particular woman, since he views women as sources of fun in his life—no more and no less. Take the mindset that of course women want you, but it's no big deal either way

5) Spread out your body.

Take up space with your arms, legs, and chest. Keep your neck straight with your back so that your head is held high.

(Something that helped me get used to keeping my neck straight was removing the pillow from my bed. After all, it's a major challenge to have optimal posture when your neck is bent for 8 hours every night.)

CHAPTER 18: Seven Steps to Create the Conditions That Increase Your Lays—Now!

What Women Find Attractive in Men ... and Why

OK, now I'm going to finally explain how to pick up and lay women to you, but before I do, I have to explain the deal with us men. Seriously.

It all boils down to two categories of guys: guys who get laid and guys who don't.

Because you're reading this book, it is likely that you're in the latter category. That's okay, because by reading this book and **applying what you learn**, you will become a man who gets laid. There is zero doubt in my mind about that.

From what you've read so far, it should be clear by now that to become a man who gets laid, you must have attractive qualities that increase the likelihood that women will find you attractive.

To understand what women find attractive in men, you must understand human biology and evolution. Men get sexually turned on by women who appear young and fertile. This is because women are at the peak of their ability to bear children until their mid 20s, after which that ability steadily declines over the next two decades until menopause.

Men, on the other hand, remain fertile well into old age. As a consequence, women tend to be a lot less interested in a man's age or the youthfulness of his appearance. What women look for instead, then, is high status, since they want an alpha male.

From the standpoint of biology and instinct, women have the desire to have sex with a dominant alpha male. Therefore by displaying high status and alpha qualities, a man can trigger a woman's biological sexual desires.

Attraction is not a choice that a woman makes consciously. It is more a biological reaction to your traits... just as your attraction to a super hot model is a biological reaction that you don't have much conscious control over.

The Simple Seven Step Seduction System

What I'm going to discuss all boils down to the following Seven Step Seduction System that takes you from saying "hello" to a new woman... to sharing orgasms in bed with her... in just one evening.

1) You will walk by a woman and have a quick, neutral conversation.
2) At the end of the conversation, you will either get her phone number to set up a date or have the interaction end right then and there with you getting rejected —and that's OK.

3) When you meet her for your date, take the mindset that you're getting to know the woman before you two have sex. Talk about neutral subjects and just vibe with her.
4) On the date, you'll start feeling horny. As the two of you continue vibing, she, too, will gradually feel horny.
5) As she gradually feels horny, you should escalate touching her, starting with her fingers, then going to her hand, to her wrist, to her forearm, to her upper back, to her upper arm.
6) When you feel the moment is right, suggest a neutral reason for the two of you to be alone together, like listening to a CD.
7) When the two of you are alone, escalate the interaction toward sex.

None of this is very complicated, and all seven steps will be discussed in more detail later.

Being Persistent

Throughout your interaction with a woman, it's vital that you take the lead. You must have a strong **will and desire** to have sex. Lack of horniness on your part can cause you to give up if the interaction becomes difficult. (Plus, it's important for you to be horny if you want her to feel that same emotion!)

Talk with a woman as long as you can. If you have to, wait for her to reject you outright rather than leaving. Countless times I have successfully hung in there through the awkwardness of a lull in the conversation rather than walking away.

The same goes when you have the woman alone with you at your place. You **must** persist through her token resistance or else you'll find yourself at best just cuddling with her all night (i.e., she gets the emotional validation of getting your devotion, while you just get blue balls.)

So the point is: make it your goal to either get laid or have her say "no" to you. Don't run away. Running is what beta males to so they don't have to get rejected.

Most men are scared to death of talking to women who they don't know, so by talking with them anyway, you separate yourself from most other guys.

You'll get rejected a lot, but that's fine. Rejection from a woman is a victory. It means that you had the guts to go for it with her.

As an alpha male, you have the strength to do what you want in life. Because you want to get laid, you will persist with the women you desire. Right? Ok, great! So remember—with women you want to have sex with, your goal is to persist until you either get laid or get rejected.

The Approach

Now I'm going to let you on one of my secrets. The woman of your dreams will never, as long as you live, knock on your front door to introduce herself to you.

That sounds obvious, but unfortunately, many guys live like that's going to happen. They never go out and talk to women, instead believing that if they work hard and make lots of money, someday fate will just bring the woman of their dreams into their lives.

Does this sound like you? Don't feel bad; it used to describe me.

The number one rule is that you, the man, must make the effort to approach women. You must go out and take the lead and work at it. Women are not going to just show up at your door.

Because they make up half of the human population, you can meet women everywhere. The rules are different for each venue, so you need to adjust yourself accordingly.

Where to meet women

As they travel throughout the day –

This is my main hunting ground. You can find women who are all by themselves at clothing stores, bookstores, coffee shops, universities, laundromats, grocery stores, malls, sandwich shops, and banks, to name a few places.

You'll have the most success approaching women who are **by themselves** and not out with friends, coworkers, etc.

This is mainly because women who are around other people are afraid the others will see them as a slut. Remember, women in general have an extremely high reverence for the opinions of other people.

Another reason to avoid women in groups is that you will often be cock-blocked—other people will interrupt the conversation, take the woman somewhere else, and do various other things to prevent you from having sex with her. Ever had a woman's friend jump in and say, "Come on, we've got to get going," and pull her away? Uh-huh.

When a woman is by herself, she acts differently from when she is with others. Even the most outgoing social butterfly will have a normal rapport-type conversation when she is by herself with you rather than entertaining a group.

Online –

Online dating can be a real opportunity for you, since a lot of guys look down on Internet dating. Thus, they aren't there to compete with you. The advantage of Internet dating is that it allows you an easy way to meet women and skip directly to the one-on-one date that leads to the lay.

Women you meet online tend to be older than college age and rarely younger than around 24. (Girls in their late teens and early 20s have so many guys to choose from in real life that few of them bother with online dating.)

With women you connect with online, try to set up a meeting as quickly as you can. Don't waste a lot of time with instant message or email chatting. Keep any phone calls as brief as you'd like, since you don't get laid on the phone. To avoid wasting your time with a fat hog, make sure you insist on seeing photographs!

You can pretty much assume the woman is attracted to you if she has agreed to meet with you, given that you've already been pre-screened by her for appearance and personality. So once you meet, it's a simple process to get laid, since you'll be alone with her.

So, the key advantage of online dating is that **it's an easy way to get laid**.

Give sites such as eharmony.com a shot. That site, in particular, has more women than men, due to a long "personality test" that most guys don't have the patience to fill out.

With eHarmony's personality test, you'll be matched up with women who have given similar answers on their tests, so answer the questions with that in mind.

(In other words, if you're looking for a quiet woman, answer the questions as if you yourself are a quiet person. If you go for a "natural salesperson" type of chick, then answer the questions that way.)

Be prepared to have your online dating experience be a numbers game. Even my best-looking friends meet no more than 5% to 10% of their eHarmony matches.

I'm at about 10%, not because of my looks, but because I've honed the things I say to the girls, so that by now what I say to them has essentially become highly-targeted direct marketing.

This brings up a point: test, test, and do more testing! The way eHarmony works is that you and your matches will be able to ask each other a series of questions.

You'll notice that on many of the questions, you'll get a better response rate if you type in your own unique answers rather than choose from the multiple choices available to you.

Try to be funny or witty with most of your answers. Only be serious with a few. Don't be negative or down on yourself at all. Remember, you're an advertiser selling a product (i.e., yourself).

Do the same thing with your profile. Where is a good source for a lot of the things you put in there? From the women's profiles! Look for some of the wittier phrasings, and then copy and paste them into your own profile. Sneaky, but effective.

Experiment with different pictures. Eharmony allows you to post multiple pictures of yourself, so take advantage of that.

Don't post "safe" looking pics of yourself with goofy, teeth-baring smiles that make you look like you're someone's Cousin Steve. Instead be a little daring with your pics. Post both action shots and shots of you chilling out. You can get a special introductory deal on eHarmony by going through this special link that I've set up with them: http://www.alphamalesystem.com/eharmony

Match.com is another great site, since it allows you to email the chicks and bypass the silly Q&A session that you must deal with on Eharmony. Keep in mind, however, that the typical chick there receives dozens and dozens of emails from guys (particularly if she's hot), so you should try to make your email stand out from the pack.

An advantage of Match.com is that it allows you to fill out an extended profile of yourself. Use this to the fullest! Write a complete sales letter for yourself, using as much text as you can get away with. Remember, women are reading your profile because you already have their attention, so they will eagerly read it to the end.

If you'd like a free 3-day trial to Match.com, go to it through this special link I've set up with the company: http://alphamalesystem.com/match

Speed dating –

This is an event that's becoming increasingly popular in urban areas. Here's how it works: about 20 single men and women take turns having 5-minute one-on-one conversations. When the five minutes are up with one girl, you move on to the next one.

I've gotten a lot of easy lays from speed dating, so I highly recommend it as a place to meet women. For some reason, these sorts of events seem to be more popular with women than men, so use that fact to your advantage.

In your conversations, don't be overly factual when you answer questions such as "What do you do for a living?" Be playful, unless you do something incredibly cool.

I really like speed dating particularly for guys who:

- a. Have trouble approaching strange women, since speed dating **forces** you to.
- b. Take their interactions with women too seriously and make themselves too nervous. When you have 5-minute conversations with ten women in the

span of 2 hours, you're going to rapidly become desensitized to what any of them think about you. Instead you'll view dating for what it ultimately is—a numbers game and no big deal at all.

You'll find the same sorts of women at speed dating events that you find on eHarmony—i.e., mid-20s and older, and just a tad desperate. Getting laid from speed dating is a piece of cake.

Weddings –

Single women go to weddings with their minds open to the possibility of meeting someone there. Try to mingle as much as you can and avoid getting drunk. You have an easy topic for initial conversation by talking about how you know the bride and/or groom. Tell interesting or funny stories about either of them if you know any.

At Work –

A great many relationships start in the workplace. In fact, it's one of the best places for people to fall in love, because they are around each other many hours of the day, under conditions that are often challenging and require cooperation and trust.

The trouble with meeting women at your workplace is that you have to tread lightly, because if you come on too strong and trigger a sexual harassment charge, you could lose your job. So the best way to handle a potential workplace romance is to make the women come to you. In other words, don't put much effort into meeting women at your job, but remain receptive to it.

Outside –

Got a dog? Walk it outside regularly in areas where there are girls. I used to take my greyhound to a park and strike up easy conversations focused on my dog. Being in a horny emotional state is important here, since you will need to change the subject and being horny will cause you to think about things other than your dog. Get phone numbers from women and call them later, since you have your dog with you and can't really go for a long interaction with them right then.

By the way, later when you're on your date with the chick, the perfect excuse for the woman to come home with you is "to meet your dog."

Bars and Nightclubs –

Sure, nightspots have a lot of hot girls concentrated in one spot. But there are so many disadvantages that they're actually one of the most difficult places to hook up with women. Having met women both in nighttime situations and in daytime, I consider the latter to be far superior.

The problem is that women in clubs get hit on by unlimited numbers of random drunk guys, so they have their defenses up—waaay up.

To make matters worse, most girls go to a club just to go dancing and hang out with friends, not to meet a guy. (It's not that they don't want to, just that usually that's not why they're there.) A good friend of mine describes women in nightclubs as acting like "retards with ADD," which isn't far from the truth.

Almost no woman goes to a nightclub by herself, so even if you do strike up a conversation with a girl, you have to contend with her friends interfering to pull her away from you. And be prepared for insane competition. Clubs are filled with jealous guys who cock-block and players who will make moves on your woman.

In clubs, be prepared to put up with behavior that you'll almost never see during the day. Because people are either drunk or have been dealing with drunks all night, they tend to be less gracious and more obnoxious and pushy.

If you want to be successful in clubs, avoid getting drunk and/or getting in fights. Both are turn-offs for women, not to mention being bad for your health!

Dress just a bit flashier than other guys (though not too much), and try to go with a wingman who can distract her friend if you chat up a group of two girls. (If you go for a set of three girls, you need to have two other guys with you to occupy both friends—or a **very** talented wingman.)

It can be very tough to separate a woman from her friends, particularly if she is young, so I can't overemphasize the importance of having a wingman to occupy each of her friends.

As long as each girl has met a guy whom they all like and trust, the group of girls will be receptive to splitting up. Otherwise, forget it—you aren't going to split them up; they all have cell phones and can find each other.

Try to go for a lay on the same night you meet a woman because you'll have much more of a challenge calling them later than you would if you met them in a daytime situation.

This is because no matter how charming you were, women always rationalize that they were drunk, so they have no idea who you were, and besides, they associate you with the swirling lights and noise of the club.

Because a nightclub is such a fake situation, try to get a woman **out of there** and into a quieter, more relaxed setting.

Ideally you'll do this immediately if not sooner (if you don't want to go home to drunkenly masturbate, that is), but since the girl needs to spend some time with you at the club before she'll go anywhere with you, do suggest a venue change as soon as you detect she's receptive to it.

Say something like, "I could sure use an omelet from that diner across the street. They've got the best omelets in the world! Let's go over there for awhile and hang out."

Remember that women at nightclubs are in party mode, so you have to frame any suggestions to go somewhere else in emotional terms as if you're going to leave the club and do something else that's equally awesome and fun.

Once you've gotten her out of the club to an eating establishment (or wherever), treat the interaction as if it were a regular date. Try to gear down the energy level until the two of you are relaxing together. (Remember, for girls to get sexual, they must be relaxed.)

And don't make out with girls in clubs even though it's tempting! Do minor touching such as holding hands and dancing, but avoid having a girl in public act in any way that that she will later think back on as having been "slutty."

Once the two of you are alone, you can make out to your heart's content, but don't go for it where other people can see.

Clubbing can wear on you. I used to go out four nights a week, every week, in order to meet women. I'd be up until 3 AM—sometimes later when I had a one-night stand.

Besides sleep deprivation, I had to inhale cigarette smoke at the clubs, plus get hearing damage from super-loud music played for the dancing drunks. And of course, there were the hangovers!

I also found that the kind of women who I like— intelligent, clever women who have more going for them than just looks—only rarely go to clubs.

So overall, when I consider the disadvantages of nightclubs, compared with the ease of approaching women in daytime who are by themselves, I really recommend skipping the nightclub scene.

Happy Hours –

This is the exception to my advice about avoiding bars and nightclubs. A bar during happy hour usually is a completely different place at 6 PM than it is at midnight.

Typically, happy hour is quiet and laid back, full of low-energy people relaxing after a hard day of work. Women in these settings are looking to unwind and de-stress. They tend to be sociable and more open than at night.

If you're an older guy, happy hour also has the advantage that you can find an older, more mature demographic of women there. These are the women who aren't able to dance till 2 in the morning anymore because they have to be at work or in class by 8 AM.

Happy hour also has the advantage of being about a couple of hours before dinner. If you hit it off really well with a woman, you can then say, "You know what? I could use a bite to eat. Let's go to this really awesome place I found last week."

House Parties -

These things can be fun. They're similar to nightclubs, except for two key advantages:

1) Everyone there has been pre-screened (since they must be friends of someone there in order to be invited to the party), so girls there will feel more comfortable around you.
2) Thanks to noise ordinances, the music can never get too loud. This enables you to have a conversation with the chick you want to lay that night.

Despite house parties having the advantage of being quieter than the typical nightclub, you're still competing with lots of distractions (keg, dancing, friends trying to get her to go to bars with them).

So your goal should still, as with nightclubs, be to get a woman out of there and into a quiet dating venue such as a diner where the two of you can be alone.

Charity events –

I find that there are surprisingly few single men at non-profit functions and tons of single women. Women love to give.

In addition to that favorable guy-girl ratio, an advantage of volunteering is that it's one of the most satisfying activities you can do.

Plus, women find men attractive who have a passion for something. One of the best things you can talk about with a woman is a chick-friendly issue that you're passionate about.

One of my big passions is animal rescue, so I volunteer at the adoption drives that my local pet store has. (Virtually all women are in favor of saving animals.)

Classes –

In terms of strategy, you want to go where the women are and where the men aren't.

Ever wanted to be the only straight male surrounded by 25 hot, sexy women? Then consider yoga class! You'll benefit from yoga by learning relaxation exercises, proper breathing, and good posture.

By the way, if can often be a challenge to make small talk with your female classmates without it being obvious to them why it is you're chatting with them.

You see, if a woman knows you're attracted to her before she feels attracted to you, then she'll feel creeped out.

So the best way to make initial conversation is to talk about the yoga (or whatever the subject of the class is) itself.

If you do yoga, try to learn all you can about the subject from web searches and whatnot. That way you can share interesting knowledge about yoga with them. Because of your expertise, you'll gain alpha status.

Other female-loaded courses include arts and crafts, cooking, writing/literature, psychology, and foreign languages. An advantage of taking a variety of courses is that you'll have things to talk about with women. I have a strong interest in psychology and try to learn all I can about it, and I've noticed that a lot of women have an interest in it as well.

Activities –

There are lots of groups out there you can join for just about anything, from singing in a choir to hiking through the woods to dancing salsa. Of course, you should skip the male-dominated events such as Trekkie conventions and chess clubs.

Figure out what your non-male dominated passions are and try them out! They may surprise you. For example, 75% of the people who do outdoor activities such as hiking and mountain climbing are women. A majority of people who are into adventure tours in foreign countries (e.g., eco-tourism to Costa Rica) are also women.

Also consider thrill-seeking activities. I have a friend who skydives quite a bit, and women drool over him because of it. If you ever want a woman to trust you completely and give herself to you, take her skydiving with you.

Conventions -

Remember how women on vacation are the easiest lays? Well, did you know that you can find hotels full of hot, horny women who are hundreds (and sometimes thousands) of miles from home?

That's right... I'm talking about conventions.

The largest profession that's absolutely **dominated** by hot women is nursing. There are millions of nurses and nursing students, who have literally hundreds of conventions a year, all over the United States (and undoubtedly the situation likely is similar in other countries).

So spend a few minutes on some search engine like Google.com and you may find a nursing convention near you scheduled soon.

Your social circle –

Talk to couples and you'll find that many of them met through their network of friends. Either they got set up, or they hung out through mutual friends and found they had a good vibe going.

So work on increasing and develop your social circle, both men and women. Call your old friends. Make new friends. Hang out with the guys from your office. Get a group together to go bowling or to a movie. The more people you know, the more introductions you'll get.

Don't get trapped into sitting around a house watching sports and drinking beer with a group of guys, however. Always make sure that you go **out** with your friends.

How to Expand Your Social Circle... Even If You're Lonely and Have Zero Friends Right Now.

You don't need to be any sort of conversational genius to make friends (and lots of them!). All you need to do to build your social network is to be **friendly** and **proactive**.

To be friendly, you need to focus on the other person's enjoyment. Be optimistic and pump them up with positive emotions. Even the nerdiest people you can imagine have friends. Mainly, you don't want to be negative... either about other people or down on yourself.

Loneliness often comes from your mindset. When someone feels insecurity, depression, and in general has a poor self image, it's no wonder few people want to hang out with them.

Remember that in the long run, people only want to hang out with you if they get a benefit from that. If you cause someone to feel negative emotions, they're going to have limited patience with you.

Also, nobody likes someone who's down on themselves and always wanting you to feel sorry for them. If you have feelings of hostility or sullenness, try to keep them to yourself.

When you're with friends, let them talk about the things that they want to talk about. Don't be needy. As an alpha male, you don't always have to tell your friends everything. You don't always have to steer the conversation towards yourself.

Next, you need to be proactive. Always assume that others are just lazy about calling you to hang out. After all, why wouldn't they want to hang out with someone as awesome as you?

Because most people are lazy, take the initiative to call your friends. Don't just expect them to call you. See yourself as the organizer of your social life. Just as you must be responsible for the sex that you have with women, you must be the one to take responsibility for everything that you do with your friends.

Other than that, there are few other guidelines for building your social circle:

1. Don't have expectations of your friends. You don't control their lives. Just accept them for who they are— what they do and how they think.
2. Also, even though you're flexible about who you hang out with, don't change your personality in order to conform to peer pressure.
3. Accept that having friends comes at a cost. If you have to leave work early in order to go to happy hour with the guys, then so be it. If you have to cut short your exam study in order to go bowling with a group

from class, then have no hesitation in doing so.

4. If you're a sociable person and have got lots of friends, be picky about who you hang out with. The wrong kind of friends can drag you down, but the right kind can pull you up. (It's better to be friends with self-made millionaires than drug-addicted street bums.)

5. If on the other hand you have no friends, don't be picky. Never say "no" when someone invites you to do something.

6. Get a cellphone. And use it. To make a new friend, simply get their phone number. And call it. Invite your new friend to come along and do something with you.

7. When you invite people to do things with you, don't make it inconvenient for them. The more convenient it is, the better. For example, if you know someone's into Star Wars movies, and there's a new one coming out that you know they'll be going to anyway, try to get them to meet you there.

8. Don't get upset if you're always the one to have to call your friends. Remember, most people lack initiative and expect others to do the work.

Finally, the main thing you never want to do in a friendship is to be needy. People won't always call you back, for whatever reason. They'll also skip out on invitations. Just be cool about it and don't let it phase you.

How to Instantly Get a Woman's Attention and What to Say When You Talk to Her

At a bare minimum, you should be able to have a basic conversation with a woman. So you should make it a rule that from now on, you'll get in at least one long, meaningful conversation a day with a woman. This can be your sister, a platonic friend, a coworker, or anyone. The main goal is to get so used to talking with women that you do it easily and naturally.

By the way, when you talk with them, don't try hard to make them feel good about you. Just have a regular conversation where you can be yourself.

To get used to talking to new women, resolve that from now on you will get into a conversation with at least four attractive women a week for the next few weeks. This can be easier than it sounds if you make sure to have something to talk about beyond just "Hi, where are you from?"

At the grocery store, say to a woman, "Hey, I need a quick female opinion. I'm buying my sister (mother, whoever) some hand cream. Which do you prefer, X scent or Y scent?" Lame, I know, but at least this will get you into conversation with a woman who you don't know.

I have by far the most success approaching women who are by themselves as they go throughout their day, so I'm going to focus on that scenario as I explain how to talk to women.

The Approach, and How to Make it

To make your approach, you need to be in the right emotional state. You need to feel a strong sexual desire and relaxed confidence. If you're nervous and fearful and struggle for things to say, the woman will find you unattractive and maybe even a bit creepy.

I know, I know…in an ideal world, women would realize that they should be flattered that a guy is struggling with what to say to them. However, as men who want to get laid, we must adjust ourselves to reality. You must be confident, horny, and relaxed-- not panicked and asexual.

Remember, every girl wants sex. Some have psychological blocks such as frigidity, but most will have sex with you if you're an alpha male, create the right conditions for sex to take place, and lead the interaction toward the lay.

Where so many guys screw up with women is by using a pick up line. The trouble with pick up lines is that they reveal to the woman right off the bat, before you've even gotten the chance to talk with her, that you feel attracted to her.

And unless you've got something going for you such as good looks, you don't want her to **instantaneously** decide whether she's attracted to you or not.

Instead it's better to come in under her radar. Display your alpha male personality, and then you can **assume attraction**. (I talk more about what it means to assume attraction below.)

Not only do you want to get under her radar, but you want to grab her attention at the same time. Get her interested in talking to you.

Finally, you want to have a **neutral** conversation with her at first. You know how you feel defensive whenever you're out walking and some bum comes up to you saying, "Hi, how are you?"

You feel defensive when that happens, because you know the bum wants your money. He's chasing rapport with you too early... since he doesn't know you, he has no reason to want to connect with you like that.

Well, it's the same sort of reaction with women. When you come up to a girl chasing rapport off the bat, her defensive shields kick in.

So instead when you have a neutral, normal conversation with the girl, she doesn't have those initial shields.

And once you have that initial conversation with a woman, as long as you keep a regular conversation and **assume rapport** (more on that later as well), then you will be eating breakfast in your underwear with her the next morning, as long as you're persistent and sexual.

For that reason, there are what I like to call Nine Hypnotic Words. They cover all the bases listed above (get under the girl's radar, grab her attention, get her interested in the initial conversation, and are totally neutral). Your number one thing to say to a girl you randomly meet is, **"Hey, I need a quick female opinion on something."**

What you get their opinion about can be extremely flexible, but make sure it's a topic that's interesting to women.

Examples:

* Something you read in the latest issue of Cosmo.

* "What do you think about this shirt?"

* "I'm thinking about buying this painting. What do you think about it?"

* "When a woman asks me whether her clothes make her look fat, what should I say?"

* Ask her about a dating situation that a male friend of yours faced with a girl. "My friend was just with this girl all day studying with her. She tore a page out of her book and threw a paper airplane at him. She was laughing, and he was having fun. Then when he went to throw it back, she all of a sudden became serious and said, 'Don't do that!' He said

the situation was awkward at that point. So he was wondering, what should he have done?"

- Ask "If your boyfriend played video games all day, how would you feel about that?" Then go into story about how your friend's girlfriend dumped him because he played his Sega too much.

- Ask what girls think about fill-in-the-blank [Mike Myers, Mick Jagger, etc.] male celebrity, such as whether girls think he's hot. Then talk about how some girl you know started stalking him (making phone calls to his publicist and planning a trip out to the celebrity's house in Beverly Hills) when she got his autograph. (At this point the girl you're chatting will tell you that the other girl is weird, and so now, congratulations, you're in conversation with a woman you met randomly on the street. You can then talk with her about what celebrities she thinks are hot, etc.)

- Start a conversation about whatever is going on at the time. For example, if you go to a dog rescue event, talk about the animals up for adoption.

- "Great weather today, huh?" (Especially if it's not!)

- "Have you tried this new kind of mint gum?" (Say this at the grocery store.) "What did you think?"

- Et cetera.

You can chat with a girl on virtually anything right off the bat, as long as it's neutral.

But be sure that it's a topic that you're interested in too. That way you come across as genuine and not like you're trying to pick them up.

Also, never recite memorized material! Just use the above list as conversation topics, not as scripts. Believe me—and it took me awhile to learn this—if you come across like a stage actor reciting lines, you'll crash and burn.

Another key point (which took me a long time to finally figure out)... When you start the conversation, make sure not to come across as **too slick** or like it's too easy to talk to her. Otherwise she will say something like, "Are you selling something?" or "Have I met you before?" Instead just be normal (though relaxed and nonchalant)!

Your main thing to talk about can be as simple as your immediate environment. If you're in a movie theater, ask her if she's ever seen a particular movie and what she thinks of it. Tell her a story about something interesting that's happened to you at a movie before.

One of my movie stories that I told one a chick I picked up from a movie theater and eventually laid:

I took one of my old girlfriends to a movie and it was just us two and these eight teenage boys. They were being all loud and jumping around before the movie started.

She had an outburst and said to them, "You had better get this out of your system right now, because when the movie starts, you need to be quiet!"

They all gave **me** the dirty looks, because as guys, you can't fight girls but you can fight other guys.

So then later on I went into the restroom and there all eight of them were. I felt like they were all about to jump me.

But then they got really whiny and said, "Don't tell on us!" It turned out they were in there hiding because they'd snuck into the movie theatre and didn't want to get caught.

I know the above story is lame, but that doesn't matter to a girl. Just be sure when you tell your stories to emphasize the emotional parts, since emotion is like crack cocaine for girls. (In the example above, it has more of an impact to use a whiny voice when imitating the teenage boys for instance.)

And also, don't use my story. Use your own!

If you're in the waiting room of a dental clinic (as I was a few months ago), ask her if she's seen that particular dentist before and what her opinion is of him (as I did with this chick who's phone number I got and saw the next day... it was a nice, standard coffee-shop-then-bar-then-my-house-then-sex-after-several-hours-on-my-couch-watching-videos kind of lay).

Tell her you're cautious these days about dentists because of this one dentist you went to named Dr. Finger who had the fattest fingers you've ever seen in your life.   (At this point she should laugh.)

From there you can talk about how you think it's interesting that people become the occupations that fit with their last name. Dr. Finger was a dentist. You also knew a girl named Amy Salmon who went into fish conservation.

At this point, if the girl is worth talking to, she will share similar weird coincidences or talk about something else to keep the conversation going. So this is a way to gauge her availability to you—i.e., whether the conversation becomes two-sided.

(A woman who doesn't make conversation with you is so not interested in you that she won't even give you a chance, or she's just nervous. If it's the latter, I like to just take the girl's phone number and see her another time, since it's difficult to have same-day sex with a nervous chick.)

Once you've made your opening comment and she replies, let the conversation flow. Change the subject. Talk about whatever else is on your mind, such as something interesting you just read in *Psychology Today*. The key is to talk about more than one subject.

Why do you want to do this? Because you want her (and you) to have the feeling that the two of you can talk about anything.

Have you ever been in a conversation like that, which seems to last for hours because you and other person keep thinking of new threads to talk about? That's the kind of rapport that you want to create.

You can always go back to previous conversational threads to reopen them and talk about them some more. This serves to give you perfect opportunity to avoid awkward pauses.

No matter what you as the alpha male decide to talk about, your attitude will be the most important thing. If you feel fear, she will detect that and be repelled by you.

Instead, approach with the full knowledge that women love sex, and so there is a good chance that a woman will appreciate you talking with her. Even if she doesn't, it's her responsibility to let you know, not yours to try to read her mind.

So have a normal conversation, be relaxed and let it flow.

The dirty little secret about your interactions with women is that it doesn't really matter what you say. You want to vibe with her and get rapport. Just get the good rapport going!

When the time comes where she asks your name, say your name with pride and give her a chance to tell you hers. If you feel like it, shake her hand at this point. This introduces the dynamic of the two of you being comfortable touching each other.

Ask her questions; make statements, and just vibe for a few minutes. You'll know she's interested in the conversation as soon as she starts making statements on her own and asking you questions back. (In other words, as I said, the conversation will become more two-sided.)

At this point, have the sort of normal conversation that you would have with an acquaintance who you'd known for a long time. (Although you haven't known this woman for more than a number of minutes, you want her to feel comfortable as if she'd known you for a while.)

When you have known somebody for long time, you don't bombard him or her with questions. Instead you make statements about what's going on around you such as how you can't believe how much junk food people are buying at the grocery store that evening.

Be laid back and vibe with her. I find that I'm a lot more successful when I'm low energy rather than high energy with a woman. The reasons are that:
1) She won't feel as if she has to work to match your emotional state if you come across as super energetic.
2) Women are more sexual when they are relaxed.

Making the Date

When the conversation has become two-sided and you feel a good vibe, it's time to seal the deal. You can either ask her out right then or get a phone number and have your date later.

Base the decision on whether the two of you have time at that point. As a general rule, it's best to avoid going on a date unless you have sufficient time to get laid. So if she's on her way to a hair appointment, get her phone number and set up the date later.

To set the date right then, make it informal and have it sound as if it's going to be quick and no big deal. Say something like, "You know, I'm in the mood for a quick cup of coffee. I'd love for you to join me."

The rules are important, so here's a summary:

1) **Give her a sense that you won't be meeting for long.** This will have a positive effect on any doubts she may have about having coffee (or whatever) with a guy she just met.

2) **Make it sound informal.** You don't want her to think of it as a date in a traditional sense, or else it will introduce a dynamic of nervousness on her part and she'll make you wait for sex. (Most women have a policy of not sleeping with a man on a first date.)

If you decide to get her phone number, just say something like, "I enjoyed talking with you, but I need to get going. Maybe we can hang out sometime."

If she makes a positive statement such as "Yeah, that would be fun," then get her digits.

As the alpha male you control the frame, so don't make a big deal out of it and she won't either.

It's always best to approach a woman who's by herself, since a woman with friends typically won't leave them to go off with some guy she's just met. (Even if she wants to, the group will interfere.)

If the women you approach is with a group, I've found that the best way to handle it is to get her phone number and set up a one-on-one meeting later.

Phone Success

In a typical relationship book, you'll find all sorts of rules like don't call for three days, etc. As an alpha male, you move through life doing whatever you want and not playing games. So, call when you want to.

In fact, I've found from experience that it's often better to call SOONER rather than LATER. Call her that night or the next day if you want to. That way, you and your conversation with her are still fresh in her mind.

When you call, you need to sound confident and comfortable with who you are. Remember, you are not imposing on her but instead giving her the honor and privilege of talking with you.

Every person is different, so there often aren't many one-size-fits-all rules for what to do when you call, but there are some basics.

One method I've found to relax and not think too much about the conversation is to do some other activity while you're on the phone. Maybe eat a bag of chips. Or call her while you're driving or walking your dog. When you're sitting by yourself in your house doing nothing, you can second-guess yourself.

When you call, a roommate or family member could answer the phone. What most guys say when they call is, in a nervous tone of voice, "Hi, is [Girl] there?"

When you do that, the automatic response of many people is to get defensive and cock-blocky and say something like (if they're polite), "Who's calling please?"

This gets you off on the wrong foot right away, and when you talk to your girl, you'll come across as nervous and therefore unattractive.

A better way to deal with the roommate or family member is to be relaxed when you call, and when someone answers, say, "Hi, this is [Your Name]. I'm giving [Girl's Name] a call."

If your girl is the one who answers the phone, that's perfect. Skip down below for where to go from there.

If it's someone other than your girl, talk easily to them and befriend them. Keep the conversation, light, cute, and funny. It will make your life an order of magnitude easier if you're friends with whomever your girl lives with.

If they tell you that the girl is not there and offer to take a message, tell them, "Thanks, but no message." Trust me, they'll tell her you called. Not leaving a message will add to your air of mystery.

Most dating advice books are wrong when they tell you to hurry to get off the phone. Unless you genuinely are in a hurry, don't feel like you have to follow such rules. Continue your relaxed frame as an alpha male. You're calling because you confidently want to chat, not because you're desperate to go on a date and think you have to pretend that you're busy.

Also, you'll find a lot of advice online about how to talk to girls on the phone, but my advice is to ignore a lot of it. Guys will have stories from their own lives and post those stories for you to adopt as your own. However, this is a huge mistake, because it comes across as fake and contrived. You should be original; talk about your own life with girls you call.

When your girl gets on the phone, do not force the conversation. Instead, simply continue the conversation you had with her when you got her phone number. Go back to those same conversational threads for a little while. When you do this, you'll get her back into the mood she was in when you met.

Then segue into telling her an interesting story about something that happened in your life.

Then tell her about a highlight from your day that girls would be interested in. Your goal is to be light and witty and just vibe with the girl.

Make sure you sound animated and non-strained; don't use a monotonous pitch or low volume voice.

Avoid talking about things that you talk about when you feel nervous. This includes things such as asking her what she's up to, asking her how her day went (instead tell her how your day went), and telling her that you're the guy who met her at the bookstore (or wherever it was).

Don't try too hard to build rapport. Instead, just assume rapport already exists. That way you can relax and have an interesting conversation.

After you've talked for awhile, meeting up with the girl will be easy. She'll probably even hint at it. Just say something like, "Hey, I'm super busy with work, but it would be fun to hang out for a little while at a coffee shop. When are you free?"

(Of course your goal is not to hang out only for a little while, but don't tell her that. The reason you tell her your time is limited is to allow her to drop her defenses about having sex on that first date.)

If she gets flaky or gives you a negative answer, don't worry about it. At least you got 10 or 15 minutes practice talking on the phone with a girl you barely know.

Just say, "Pleasure chatting with you. I guess I'll talk to you later." Don't end by saying, "Hey, I'll call back you this weekend." The first keeps you as more of a challenge and unpredictable in her eyes.

The Date

When you're talking with a woman one-on-one, it's time to slowly escalate the interaction toward sex. Realize that the woman wants sex just as much as, if not more than, you do. There are four things you will focus on:

1) Being relaxed as much as possible (i.e., the opposite of nervous and unconfident).

2) Feeling sexual and horny.

3) Talking like you're old friends.

4) Taking the lead and persisting towards the lay.

The only place you should ever take a woman on a first date

Take her to a place that's not traditionally associated with "romance."

By that I mean, don't take her to a fancy dinner or do anything else that she associates with a "date." If you do, that puts her into the same "make him wait" mindset that she adopted with the last 100 guys who bought her a nice dinner.

Instead meet her somewhere informal, like a coffee shop or some cheap diner for lunch. Don't make a big deal out of who pays for what, because again, the last 100 guys she dated paid for her meal because, as was blatantly obvious to her, they were hoping to get laid.

As an alpha male, you shouldn't do anything because you're "hoping to get laid." That reeks of desperation and kills attraction that a woman feels.

(A more attractive guy is one who gets laid all the time, so sex is no big deal to him. If a woman wants his attention, she has to earn it... not the other way around. In other words, he is a challenge for her, not a sure thing.)

Like I said much earlier, spending money on a woman lowers your value in her eyes. So avoid the money issue when thinking of places to take the girl. Yet at the same time, you don't want to appear cheap.

My favorite place to meet is at a coffee shop, because it's casual, a very public place where women feel safe, and a place where it's never necessary to spend more than a few bucks. So if you decide to buy her coffee, it's never a big deal.

Another big advantage to meeting for coffee is that it avoids the intense dating frame where everyone's nervous, such as when you go for dinner on a first date, since a coffee shop is such a relaxed, comfortable venue.

Relaxation should be a big factor in deciding where to take a girl. If the place is too fancy, then it becomes intimidating. Remember, for a woman to become receptive to sex, she needs to feel relaxed.

Another option is a combination restaurant and bar such as Applebee's or Chili's. That makes it easy and natural to proceed from the meal to the bar.

Try to go to a place that's near your house. The longer the journey is from the meeting locale to your pad, the longer the time window the woman has to fall out of her horny emotional state and start thinking bad thoughts about how she's on her way to the house of a man she's on a first date with.

Another thing to consider... become a regular customer at wherever you want to take girls. In my case, I'm a regular at a coffee shop not far from my house. Tip the employees well. Get them to like you.

That way, when a girl goes to the venue with you, she'll see that the people there know you and like you, which increases your social status in her eyes.

Girls place a lot of emphasis on a guy's social status. So it helps you when the girl sees that other people know you and like you. To her, that means you're normal instead of some creepy weirdo.

Another suggestion, while we're on the subject of your social status, is to take girls to any place you are popular or people defer to you. If you're the boss at work, for example, have the girl come there to meet you before going to your date. (See page 33 for more on this.)

When taking your seat at the dating locale, do the opposite of what the etiquette books tell you. Rather than have the woman sit on the seat by the wall, you should take it.

Have your back to the wall. Have her sitting across the table from you, so that all she can see is you and the wall. This minimizes the distractions that you have to compete with.

You'd rather have her focus on you, rather than compete with the other people she'd see in the diner/ coffee shop, the view of the river, or buildings across the street, other people in the dating locale, etc. You do not want her attention to be interrupted by anything that's more interesting than you.

By the way, throughout this, notice I've been talking about where **you** want to go. This is an important point. You want to control the frame. Let her enter your world, not the other way around.

So don't be like the weak-willed guys who say, "Where would you like to meet?" Have a place in mind, and **bring her into your reality**.

Later on in the relationship, this can and must change. But early on, always have a place in mind where you want to go and take on this mindset: "I'm going to be doing something fun, and this woman is merely coming along for the ride."

How to Make Easy and Successful Conversation on a Date

You want your conversation to be free flowing and unforced, so keep your discussion informal the way you would talk with a friend. Take the mindset that you're patiently getting to know her a bit before the lay. Be relaxed and don't think too much about what to say.

Here are some suggestions for what to talk about:

- **Interesting stories from your life.** She will probably also start talking about interesting stuff from her own life. If something she says fascinates you, tell her you'd like to hear more about it. However, do not fake interest in something, since women can often detect phoniness.

- **Highlights from the past few days of your life.** Make these emotionally relevant, such as something cool that you saw, or something that was outrageous or out of place that happened. She will probably tell her own highlights.

- **TV shows, movies, and celebrities.** Even if you don't spend much time watching TV, you can become knowledgeable fast by spending a few minutes checking out CNN Entertainment at www.cnn.com/SHOWBIZ and MSN Entertainment at entertainment.msn.com. The Hollywood A

List website at www.thehollywoodalist.com is a good source for celebrity gossip that you can make easy conversation about with most women.

- **Music.** Check out *Rolling Stone* magazine to get up to speed both on what music is hot right now and how you can talk about music in a way that sounds interesting.

- **Food.** No matter whether a woman is fat or thin, the odds are high that she's positively *obsessed* with this subject.

- **Vacations.** Talk about cool aspects of places you've been to.

- **Your passions in life.** You *do* have passions, do you not? If not, develop some. And develop the ability to talk about them.

- **Differences between men and women.** Many girls can talk for hours about this!

- **Shoes.** Women have a peculiar fascination with them, and you can easily have a half hour's worth of conversation with just about any woman merely by having her educate you about shoes.

It's okay to ask her questions about herself, but try to avoid doing it too much. Why? Because you usually don't ask a lot of questions when you're talking to someone you know. (And remember, you're trying to create within her the feeling that "This guy's so easy to talk to, it's as if I've known him for ages!")

When finding out information, make statements instead of asking questions.

It's fine to ask, "What kinds of books do you like to read?" But a better way to phrase it is, "I'd love to hear about what kinds of books you read."

This communicates your vibrancy and is a more personal statement, since you're expressing your feelings and reactions.

What you talk about isn't important, since a woman won't have sex with you simply based on what you say. However, she will screen you out if you talk about the **wrong** things.

Lots of guys screw this up, so pay close attention to this list of 14 specific topics you should never, ever bring up in conversations with a woman you want to have sex with:

1) **Negative things such as how much she hates her job.**

Keep the interaction positive. You want her to associate *good* feelings with you.

Besides, you're the man who will have sex with her, not be her psychologist! Let her friends listen to her problems instead of you.

If she brings up negative stuff, steer the conversation to stuff you prefer. To be nice, before you change the subject, say something like, "I'll help you take your mind off that."

2) **Sharply negative things about yourself**.

Don't tell her how you spent two years in state prison, how much you hate your dead-end job, or how you're a shy person who doesn't date much.

However, she knows no one's perfect, so you **should** disclose minor vulnerabilities from time to time, such as how you get nervous when you give a speech in front of large crowds[8], how you're bad about keeping your car clean[9], or how you've always been afraid of the thought of your parents dying[10].

Talking about minor vulnerabilities can increase her affection for you because
        a. It personalizes you and helps her relate to you.
        b. It demonstrates that you're not trying to win her approval.

3) **Controversial things.**

Sorry, gunslinger. If she gets riled up about the number of people who own guns, sex will be the last thing on her mind.

---

[8] You'll almost always get a "Me too!" reaction when you tell her this.

[9] For some reason, most girls couldn't care less how trashed your car is. They only really care about how clean your house is.

[10] This is another vulnerability you can disclose that's guaranteed to have a woman say, "Me too!"

Also, it's possible that you hold views that would disqualify you in her mind (like maybe she's has strong views about gay marriage... and it's the opposite of the way you feel). So avoid mentioning anything with that potential.

If the woman herself brings up religion or politics, try to agree with her as much as you can. Don't be spineless and compromise on your core issues, but at the same time, even if you disagree with her, you can just say something like, "That's a good point you made. I like that you're well informed when it comes to those things. Hey, you know what?" . . . and then change the subject to something else.

4) **Topics that tend to be boring to women.**

Probably one percent of women or less *truly* give a rat's as about whether the New York Yankees will trade their overpriced pitched for Boston's steroid-addicted outfielder, so save that conversation for your night out with the guys.

Women also don't care about the new hydraulic-turbo-manifold-tune-up-charger you got on your car.

Nor are they interested in how you wasted 100 people in Grand Theft Auto... or any other computer or electronics related conversational topic, for that matter.

5) **Any technical topic.**

Save discussions of your 1 GB RAM upgrade until you're with your nerdy male friends. If you feel the need to explain what RAM is and how it works, again, save it for your bros.

I can't say this enough, but it must be drilled into your brain: **For women to get into a sexual mindset, they *must* be engaged emotionally.** When you engage them logically, it stifles the emotional sector of their mind. So don't be boring!

6) **Vulgar topics**.

You don't make yourself more sexually attractive when you explain to her that you don't want cream in your coffee because it gives you diarrhea. (Sadly, that's a real example from one of the guys I coached... amazingly to me, he had no idea that was why the chick lost interest in him!)

Also don't laugh about how you can fart on command. Women do not think things like that are funny—it grosses them out.

7) **Topics that would be offensive to women.**

There are some significant male-female differences in certain topics. Just about every woman... even the most drug addicted, self-centered party chick... has a strong nurturing instinct.

It's cool for example if you enjoy the thrill of deer hunting, but don't share that thrill with women.

Sometimes, of course, this should be obvious. A friend of mine actually told a woman how he thought it was funny when he ran over a squirrel and it was on the road flopping around. (Needless to say, he went home by himself that night.)

8) **Her ex-boyfriend or any other guys she may still like.**

When this comes up, change the subject IMMEDIATELY IF NOT SOONER.

Even if the woman talks about how she hates her ex, that means she still feels attraction for him. (If she weren't still attracted, she'd be totally indifferent to him and not want to talk about him.)

The bottom line is that you want thinking about you, and only you, not other guys.

9) **Sex.**

Do not verbalize anything about sex, because that will trigger the portion of her mind that's been trained to think, "Uh oh, this guy's after just one thing. I'd better make him wait or else people will think I'm a slut!"

If she brings up sex, just acknowledge it and talk and laugh about it like it's no big deal, and then change the subject.

Be horny, but don't verbalize anything about sex, and as you vibe with her, wait for her to gradually become as horny as you. (I will explain this concept further in the next section.)

10) **Indicators of low status.**

See the chapter on "How to be Likable" for more things to avoid talking about such as bragging about yourself.

11) **Constantly barraging her with questions.**

If you **try** for a connection rather than just acting as if it already exists, you are likely to fail. Why? Because by acting like someone who she just met, you'll be placed into that category, which makes sex that much more of a distant possibility.

Instead, you want her to think of you as the guy she hit it off with right from the start. So talk about the sorts of things that you'd talk about if the two of you were comfortable around each other and trusted each other completely.

When you're comfortable with someone, you don't barrage them with constant questions. Instead you just make statements and have normal conversations. So it should be the same with a woman.

12) **Anything that is scripted.**

If you do a web search, you can find web sites that purport to give you the ability to hypnotize women or otherwise alter their emotional states. They include canned phrases and stories designed to make women laugh and fall into a quasi-hypnotic state.

I'm not saying that stuff doesn't work, but the problem is that unless you have **extremely good** delivery, you will come across as phony if you start spouting lines at her.

The methods in this book are much simpler and will do as good a job getting you laid as any other system.

Why spend countless hours memorizing scripts when you can simply make yourself attractive and then **be yourself** with women?

13) **Romantic talk.**

You heard that right. Recite Shakespeare poems in English class, not when you're on a date.

Any romance should come after sex, not before. If you set the frame of romance, then the woman will be more likely to make you wait for sex.

Since you're a dominant male who controls the frame, you prefer to set up the dynamic where sex is a given and **no big deal**, not something that you have to suffer through months of blue balls for before the big day of deflowering comes.

14) **Too much humor.**

It's good to be naturally witty and funny in the course of your conversation, and lots of guys who are good with women are good at making them laugh.

However, don't overdo it. If you use too much humor, then the woman won't take you seriously nor view you sexually.

Remember that you control your interaction with a woman, so you want to set the right frame of mind. You're a sexual man and an alpha male, not a clown or entertainer.

Making Emotionally Relevant Conversation

When you talk to a woman, it's important to appeal to her emotions. Simply put, a woman with her emotions engaged is more receptive to sex.

For example, rather than say "I drove 5 miles just now," the way you would to one of your guy friends, you should say to her, "You wouldn't believe what I saw on my drive earlier!" (She'll get excited and ask you what it was.)

The best way to learn how to speak to a woman in an emotionally relevant way is to just talk about your daily experiences with them in a way that lets them feel the way you must have felt.

Were you yelled at by your boss? Did you notice something interesting that someone did while you were walking on the sidewalk? Did you embarrass yourself this morning in front of a lot of people?

Things like that… where you **felt** a strong emotion at the time (no matter what that emotion was) … are the kinds of conversational threads that appeal to chicks.

Remember elsewhere in this guide where I recommended that you have at least one good conversation with a woman everyday? One of the benefits you'll get from that is learning the kinds of topics that fascinate women. Eventually, emotionally relevant topics will come naturally to you.

It's also helpful to hang around women and check out how they themselves talk with once another. Then you can talk to them in a similar way. (However, make sure to be masculine about it, so you don't come across at their "gay best friend.")

The Importance of Laughter

For women, laughter can be a bonding experience, so be the guy who makes her laugh sometimes. I'm not saying be a non-stop comedian, but instead make witty observations from time to time.

By the way, never **act** witty, funny, or playful. Instead **be** those things. Develop your intelligence and make playful comments and witty observations as you please.

And realize that even if something's just a tad bit funny, the woman will laugh simply because the two of you are in rapport.

A Flirting Skill That Comes Naturally to Women But Most Guys Have Trouble With... Master This, And You'll Separate Yourself Above The Pack.

Teasing. By that I mean, sending mixed messages. Women tease guys because they love it so much.

Women tease with their eyes, looking flirtatiously at guys and then averting their glance. They tease with the way they dress, wearing outfits that reveal just so much, but not too much.

The ultimate in teasing is performed by strip club dancers. They'll grab a guy's necktie and them move in so close they're almost kissing him. Then all of a sudden they snap backward and turn their back on him. Then they repeat the process.

Think of how strippers get you excited and then withdraw, get you excited, and then withdraw.

Women do this all the time, on a number of levels.

And women do it because they realize that foreplay begins long before you reach the bedroom.

So tease a woman playfully, because she absolutely adores it. Tease her about...
- Her answers to your questions.
- The way she dresses.
- Her quirks and mannerisms.

Slap her in the ass when she says something bratty. Ball up a paper straw wrapper and throw it at her, with a mischievous grin on your face.

Frame the whole interaction with a woman almost like you're her big brother and she's your comical little sister. Keep everything funny and playful.

Matching Emotions

Hey, ever noticed how emotions are contagious? Maybe you hung around with a good friend of yours who was depressed. Then before long, you too were feeling a little down.

Or, have you ever had a time when a coworker you spent a few hours with was in a bad mood that day? You too were dragged into that mood, unless you made a special effort to stay upbeat.

The idea that emotions are contagious has profound implications. It means that a person in a group with the strongest emotion can, merely by feeling that emotion, get others into that same mood. Like a cold, people will catch the dominant person's emotions (either negative or positive).

I know this sounds crazy, but there is some compelling research to support the notion.

- One study examined two people beginning a conversation. After the first couple minutes, their heart rates matched. By the end of the 15 minutes, they not only are mirroring each other's body language, but they report feeling the same moods.
- Researchers have found that emotions spread from one person to another even when the

interaction is completely non-verbal. The one who is most emotionally expressive non-verbally ends up influencing the mood of the other person.

- In a large study of work teams in 70 different industries, researchers found that people who sat together in meeting rooms ended up sharing moods within 2 hours.
- Other longer-term studies have found that over the course of several days and weeks, people who are around each other (such as sports teams) end up harmonizing their emotions.

A lot of this comes from human evolution. As we developed into advanced primates over the past two million years, we lived in tribes or extended families.

In order to maintain cohesion, the group would look to the leader as the emotional guide. The leader pushed the group's emotions upward into soaring morale and thus the tribe was able to defend against saber-toothed tigers and other human tribes.

I found this absolutely fascinating, because the research indicates means that all you have to do is feel a strong emotion (determined yet lighthearted optimism, let's suppose) that you want another person to feel. Then you cling to that emotion as hard as you can.

As time goes on, the other person will find themselves gradually feeling more determined yet lightheartedly optimistic. (Are you beginning to see how you can apply this phenomenon with women? If not, keep reading... it will soon become clear to you!)

Books such as <u>Primal Leadership</u> by Daniel Goleman (the man who first introduced the concept of emotional intelligence a few years ago) have focused on emotion matching when it comes to leadership.

And by the way, definitely check that book out, because it will help you advance in your career. (The studies listed above were all discussed in <u>Primal Leadership</u>.)

But what does all this mean for you getting laid? What it means is that all you have to do is to **feel horny and relaxed** when talking with a woman. If the two of you get into a strong vibe and rapport, she will also feel sexually excited as time goes on.

That is the key to your date with a woman. Feel relaxed and sexual, and keep her in conversational rapport with you until she matches your emotions.

Suppose you go to a coffee shop. As you feel yourself in the sexual state, sit and talk with the woman about neutral subjects that she would be interested in. Your goal is to give the girl a window into your world.

Vibe with her, and once she feels sexually excited enough, you create the conditions for sex to take place.

Her Attraction Signals

I probably don't need to list the attraction signals that you find in relationship books. The reason is that if a woman is sticking around talking to you and being pleasant, obviously she doesn't dislike you!

But it's always possible that she likes you only as a friend (though unlikely as long as you keep pushing the interaction forward), so my advice is to learn and memorize the following list that I've come up with, and then **try to forget it**.

This is because you'll paralyze yourself during conversations if you start analyzing small details such as how forcefully she twirls her hair around her fingers.

Once you get enough experience with women, you'll recognize attraction signals instinctively. The following list is in no particular order.

1. She compliments you on just about anything.
2. She feels nervous around you. Look for signs of nervousness such as her muscles twitching.
3. She teases you playfully.
4. She makes an effort to tell you how much she **loves** the same things you like.
5. She talks about things that you guys can do in the future. "You like vintage clothing stores too?" she might say, "We should go sometime!" By the way, this is also something you should bring up with girls. Don't make it too serious though. Make it like you're being playful. "We could go shopping for the most pimp looking

purple tights on 5th Avenue!" (Say anything playfully absurd that the two of you could do in the future. Keep it verbally non-sexual of course.)

6. When her legs are crossed, look at the foot of her top leg. If it is pointed toward you, it is a sign you've got her full attention.

7. She makes an effort to keep the conversation going when it lulls. (Every once in awhile you can even test her attraction by purposely allowing the conversation to pause on your end. Then see if she restarts the conversation.)

8. She touches her face. When a person touches his or her face, it's a sign that they're thinking about something. So in order to be sure that she's thinking good thoughts, look for this signal to be combined with others from this list.

9. She gazes into your eyes and holds her gaze.

10. She mirrors you. (Being passive by nature, women will follow the lead of a man they feel attracted to.) Watch to see whether she

- Has a similar posture to yours.
- Adjusts the volume of her voice to match yours.
- Adjusts the rate of her voice to match yours.
- Matches the pace of your breathing.
- Laughs when you laugh.

11. Stroking a cylindrical object such as a wine glass or pen up and down with her thumb and

pointer finger. This means you're having a strong effect on her, big guy!

12. She tosses her head back or side-to-side. Watch for her hair to sway as she does it.

13. She touches her face while looking at you.

14. She dangles her shoe off her foot or even takes it off.

15. She rubs her fingertips around her upper chest.

16. She rubs her palm on the back of her head, causing her hair to fluff out.

17. She plays with her hair while looking at you.

18. She displays a genuine smile rather than one that's forced.

19. Her eyes sparkle because her pupils are big and dilated.

20. She raises her eyebrows at times.

21. Her nipples are hardening. Of course, you can only tell this if she's wearing the right clothes.

22. She has a relaxed face. (However, sometimes a non-relaxed face can be okay, such as when a woman is so attracted to you that she feels nervous.)

23. She gazes into your eyes. Her pupils dilate (enlarge).

24. She focuses all her attention on you, even when there are other people around.

25. She touches you while talking to you, even if it is "accidental." Women are highly conscious of their bodies, so it will rarely really be an accident when they touch you. Look for her to touch your arm to emphasize a point or brush

her foot against yours when she laughs at one of your witty statements.

26. She laughs at your comments as if they're the funniest things she's ever heard, even if they're only mildly witty.

27. She shows her tongue, like when when she touches it to her front teeth or licks her lips.

28. With her body turned towards you, she suddenly sits upright, with her arm muscles tensed and her breasts pushed out.

29. She displays her palms to you. Open palms indicate she feels open with you.

30. She rubs her wrists or plays with her bracelet.

31. Her skin becomes flushed. Look particularly to notice whether she blushes. (This can also be a signal that she feels horny.)

32. She rubs her earlobes or plays with her earrings.

33. She asks you questions about yourself. They won't just be the superficial questions that she'd ask anyone ("Where are you from?"), but instead will be deeper questions to find out what makes you tick (e.g., "What are your passions in life?")

Easy Alpha Male Exercise - Anticipate the deep questions. Have good answers prepared for them. Below are some questions you should know the answer to. (By the way, these are also good questions for you to ask a woman.)

What do you want out of life? What are your goals?

What do you like to do for fun?

What's the most embarrassing moment you've had?

What's something about yourself that most people would never guess?

34. She's energetic about talking with you.

35. Her voice becomes a little bit lower (half an octave or so).

36. She tucks in her blouse.

Below are some body language signals a woman gives out to indicate that she's not interested in you.

Usually these signals are subconscious; the woman doesn't even think about them. Sometimes women do these in an exaggerated manner to try to give you a hint.

Keep in mind though that you need to look for several of these signals being displayed before you draw any conclusions. Sometimes a person crosses their arms simply because they're cold rather than uncomfortable.

Also, try to get a woman to **verbalize** her rejection of you. On multiple occasions, I've had a woman send me rejection signals, yet I persisted in the conversation and eventually got the lay.

1. A limp hand.
2. She looks away from you, especially when you're talking to her.
3. Making little effort to talk with you. Giving one-word answers.
4. Folding her arms across her chest.
5. Crossing her legs at the ankles.
6. Continually scratching her nose. When a person feels uncomfortable, blood rushes to their nose, causing it to itch.
7. When you turn your body language toward her, she leans back and away from you.
8. She seems unenergetic about talking with you.
9. She'll have a neutral tone of voice.

Now I'm going to make things easy for you: just assume at all times that the woman is attracted to you. So much in interpersonal relations is a self-fulfilling prophecy based on our attitudes, so use that to your advantage.

If you have a strong inner attitude that says, "Of course she is attracted to me," then she will pick up on your vibe and be influenced by it.

Why You Should Assume Attraction

A lot of the advice about picking up girls found around the internet says that you should do various tactics to make a girl attracted to you. Tell memorized stories and other routines to get her laughing and so forth.

The trouble with all of this work to build a woman's attraction is that it comes from a beta male mindset. **If you're always trying to say the correct thing to a woman, then you're trying too hard for her approval**.

The fact is, if you've got good body language, strong confidence, have improved your appearance, and have a lot going on in your life, you're automatically going to be more attractive to a woman than 95% of the guys out there. (And make no mistake about it... if you're in the top 5% of male attractiveness, virtually all women will find you potentially fuckable.)

If you assume attraction, then you're going to act the correct way at all times anyway.

For example, when a woman acts bratty and asks you some question like, "Why did you decide to talk with me?" or "Do you say that kind of stuff to all the girls?" the best thing to do is to **not** search for the best answer.

Instead the best way to react is with indifference. That way you remain in control of the frame. (Whenever you care about what a girl thinks, that gives her the control.)

There's never a need to feel as if you need to entertain a woman. In fact, doing so makes you beta.

When you converse with a woman, **interact** with her. Screen her to be sure that she can keep a conversation going with you. That makes you the alpha male.

As you always assume the woman's attracted to you, the most important rule for keeping control of the frame us to always be willing to walk away.

Even though I talk about persistence until you either get rejected or laid, sometimes it's good to be the one to walk away first (if it's a girl you don't like), just to know that you can.

Being always willing to walk away if need be keeps you as a **challenge** for the girl. If a woman views a guy as a challenge, that keeps him interesting. It means she has to work for him, and if she gains his affections, that's her reward.

If you're ever a "sure thing" for a woman, that gives her validation and causes her to lose attraction for you. So if you simply assume attraction, that ensures that the woman always thinks that she's more attracted to you than you are to her.

Your Behavior

Because you feel horny and want her to feel horny as well, you should **sit as close as possible to her**. According to anthropologist Edward Hall, friends tend to communicate from a distance of greater than

18 inches apart. People who are intimate with each other keep a distance of less than 18 inches apart.

Because you are creating an intimate dynamic with the woman you're dating, you should keep a close distance between the two of you. **Aim to always remain within that 18-inch intimate space.**

As you establish the dynamic of being within each other's personal space, **you also want the two of you be comfortable touching each other**.

Although you'll be touching her for ostensibly innocent reasons, human communication research has shown that a person is more likely to accept touch from another person if they feel affection toward them.

So by touching the woman, you are:
1) Triggering the parts of her mind that say, "I like this guy!"
2) Testing her to see if it's worth pursuing anything with her.

If she reacts negatively, then you know you're wasting your time hanging out with her.

It is also a hallmark of alpha males that they feel free to touch others. So by being free with your touching, you are non-verbally communicating that you are an alpha male and a man who has confidence with women.

(After all, only a man with a high degree of self-confidence can be relaxed as he touches a woman.)

Touch the woman as if it's completely natural. Don't make a big deal out of it. If she knows that it's a big deal to you (like maybe you're looking at your hand as you touch her), then the dynamic becomes one of you actively **trying** to get laid with her, which causes her defensive shields to go up.

When you're in public with her, progress like this:

1) **Touch her hand.**

You can do this in a fun way by having a thumb-wresting competition. If you don't know how to do this, watch the Arnold Schwarzenegger movie <u>True Lies</u> for the scene where he and Jamie Lee Curtis say, "One, two three, four, I declare a thumb war."

Once you've started the idea that touch can be fun like this, then you can touch her hand during other times, like when you want to find out about that cool ring she's wearing.

2) **Touch her wrist.**

Do this by noticing her watch or bracelet and commenting on it as you touch her wrist.

3) **Touch her forearm.**

Touch this when you're emphasizing a point.

4) **Touch her upper arm.**

Do it when you're telling her something interesting that you just thought of.

5) Touch the back of her head.

Do this in the context of you whispering a fun secret into her ear.

(At this point, the two of you should be comfortable enough touching each other that you can hold her hand.)

6) Touch her lower back.

Touch her there when you two stand up and you start walking out of the dating location with her.

The number one thing to do throughout the entire process, in case I haven't emphasized it enough, is to be relaxed.   Sit laid back and spread out.

To stay relaxed, view the interaction with the woman as not being all that important.

All you're doing when you're talking with her and hanging out to get to know her and establish a connection before you have a more physical "connection" with her.

Gaze into her eyes when you're talking. Soften your eyes in a sexual manner.

Speak in a soft, normal tone of voice as if you've been in a relationship with her for a year and feel totally comfortable around her... in other words, talk to her in a soft, sexual voice.

Use The Powerful "Boyfriending Technique"

I'm going to reveal an important comfort-building technique you won't find anywhere else. I call it "Boyfriending." In a nutshell, there's something you can do that's usually done ONLY by a woman's boyfriend.

If you do it too, it's a way of getting under a woman's radar and making her comfortable enough around you so that she'll be receptive to sex without making you wait.

You see, in order for a typical woman to have sex with a man, she must have feelings of comfort. It is not enough for her to simply feel attraction for the guy.

Let's say you meet a girl at a 5 PM happy hour. The two of you hit it off, having a great conversation. She's laughing. She's interested. You entrance her by telling her fascinating stories about your life. The two of you have good rapport.

Around 7:30, you get hungry and invite her to get something to eat. Dinner goes well too. Then dinner ends. Now what?

Around this time, a lot of guys get confused about how to advance the interaction forward. Clearly the goal is to get laid, but the roadmap is often muddled.

Usually the night ends with the woman saying something like, "I had great time meeting you. Call me. Bye!"

Often, the **need for comfort** is why women like to make guys wait before sex.

(If the guy's lucky, it might be only three dates, but with a lot of women, the guy can be made to wait for months, as we discussed earlier.)

Fortunately, there's a way to shortcircuit that barrier. I call it the "**Boyfriending Technique**."

If you watch couples who are in close relationships, you'll notice an interesting phenomenon. The man and woman are extremely comfortable touching each other, so much so that they'll even do seemingly gross things like brush sleep ("eye boogers") out of each other's eyes.

It's a behavior that's only done by people who are completely comfortable around each other. Certainly when you are in a relationship where you can brush sleep out of a woman's eye, you've long since passed the point where the two of you are comfortable having sex.

Catch my drift? You can use this as a psychological weapon to make the woman feel more comfortable around you.

In mid-conversation, tell her to hold still and close her eyes. Pretend there's sleep in her eye, and make her believe that you just brushed it off.

Later, after the two of you finish eating and leave the restaurant, again tell her to hold still. With your finger, brush off an imaginary piece of food from her lower lip.

The net result of the Boyfriending Technique is nuclear. First, it sub-communicates that the two of you are very comfortable around each other.

Second, it involves you touching her face, bringing your heads closer together and progressing towards a make out session.

Third, in the case of you touching her lower lip, you're in fact touching an erogenous zone. That's right... a woman's lower lip has a high concentration of nerve endings. Stimulating her lower lip makes her body release sex hormones.

Make the Boyfriending Technique a part of your dating arsenal, and you'll find more success than ever before. You may just be having sex within several hours instead of having to wait several months.

How to Tell When the Time is Right to Seize the Opportunity to Get Her Alone With You

As the woman feels comfortable with you and has an easy rapport with you, she will find herself feeling more and more sexual. Watch her gradually go into a horny state herself.

Watch for these eight silent clues that scream, "I want you inside me now!":

1) She looks at your mouth and then back at your eyes.

2) Her eyes are moist and glistening.

3) She touches her mouth.

4) She rubs her neck.

5) The skin of her face alternates between flushing and going pale.

6) Her eyes wander down to your genital area

7) She smoothes her skirt or the legs of her pants

8) She stares at you with a hungry look in her eyes.

By now it should be obvious what's on both of your minds. At this point, it's time to get her out of the dating location (coffee shop, diner, bar, etc.) and into a place where the two of you will be alone.

However, you do **not** want to say: "Let's go have sex!" On a first date, the easiest way to snap a woman out of her horny state is to verbalize your desire to have sex with her.

Instead, say something innocent and non-sexual to get the two of you alone together. Examples that have worked for me are:

- "You know, that's awesome about your complete collection of Prince CDs you were telling me about. I don't have much time, but I'd love to drop by and listen to a song or two."

- "I need to go by my house real quick to walk my dog. It would be great if you came along too because I'd like you to meet her."

- "I can only drop by for a few minutes, but I'd love to see how that robot vacuum cleaner of yours works."

As long as a woman is sufficiently horny, she will agree to go to a location where you can be alone. This usually will be either her place or yours. Generally women feel more comfortable in their own home.

The excuse that you use to get the two of you alone is unimportant. I like to use fake time limitations ("I only have a few minutes") to overcome any objections that they may have.

Plus there is a legitimate-sounding **innocent** reason for the two of you to be together ("You'll love my stamp collection.").

As you move to your new location where the two of you can be alone, ideally you'll be able to keep her talking and in her horny state. You don't want her to have time to think about what she's doing or to call a friend who will talk her out being alone with you.

For this reason, I like to date women at a coffee shop that's within easy walking distance of my house. That way I can hold hands with them as we walk to my place "for a few minutes."

How to Make a Woman Comfortable and Horny Enough for Sex

You want the sex to appear to her as if it happened spontaneously. After all, she was only going to come to your place for a few minutes, right?

Whether you go to your place or hers, keep the conversation going no matter what's happening. When you get out of the car in the parking lot or driveway, keep the conversation going.

As you walk through the door, keep talking. That way you keep her engaged emotionally.

Don't let the conversation pause, or else she will start to think, and when she thinks about the situation, logic might then overcome emotion, in which case you'll hear the dreaded words, "I need to get going."

At this point, you need to get her comfortable with the idea of the two of you being alone and in isolation.

If you're at her place, be overly fascinated with her library of books and collection of DVDs. If you're at your place, show her all the cool and interesting stuff you have.

You do have cool and interesting stuff at your place, right? If not, get some stuff! Basically anything that you can have a conversation about is good to have on display:

- Coffee table books about places you've traveled to.
- Artwork done by your great aunt.
- Interesting magazines (you want to have interesting ones to talk about, so think *Psychology Today* and *Entertainment Weekly*, not *Maxim* and *Playboy*!)
- Plants. Two hard-to-kill plants that look good are the jade tree and the cast iron plant.

And keep your place picked up. Not necessarily like something out of *Queer Eye for the Straight Guy*, but at least something that wouldn't fail an inspection by the health department.

Have paintings on your wall rather than posters. Have clean sheets on your bed. Have decent furniture. Vacuum and sweep your floors. Do your dishes.

As you show her around your place, you can have conversations about every room.

Easy Alpha Male Exercise:
Go around your house and think of one or two conversational threads you can have in each room; e.g., "You wouldn't believe how I ended up owning that sculpture in the corner . . ."

A friend of mine gave me a good tip about the bedroom—namely, that you should avoid calling it the "bedroom." Why? Because the word "bedroom" triggers that portion of her mind that's been programmed by our puritanical society to say, "Uh oh! Sex alert!"

So instead call it something else. My friend calls his bedroom the "meditation room."

I've started doing that too (you can even smile slyly when calling it that, which may get a giggle out of her), and talking about how I like to go my mediation room to have quiet contemplation sometimes.

Find an excuse for the two of you to sit very close to each other in your living room or bedroom.

I like to say, "Check out my photo album, I've got some awesome picture from my blah-blah vacation," after which we're sitting hip-to-hip on my couch as I flip through the interesting pictures.

Movies are fantastic. They give you an hour and a half of time on the couch with her to progress towards sex. So put on a movie if you can.

It can be pretty much any kind of movie, but I find light comedies such as Ghostbusters to be best.

By the way, Ghostbusters is a great movie to watch with a girl you've just brought home because: 1) It's a movie that just about everyone has fond memories of, yet it's been several years since they've seen it.

2) There is a **lot** of sexual innuendo in the film.

One of the best preludes to sex you can be in with a woman is the standard "make out" position on a couch. The two of you are sitting together hip to hip, you with your arm resting behind her on the back cushions.

Let some time pass. Sexually, a woman is like an iron. She slowly heats up. A man, by contrast, can turn his horniness on and off almost like you'd turn a light on and off.

So what you need to do is have her slowly heat up. Gradually progress from one stage to the next. Make sure not to move faster than she is able to heat up, or else the sex will not happen.

At some point, lightly touch her shoulder with your hand and then pull it back. Awhile later, put your hand more firmly on her shoulder. If she's interested in you, she'll snuggle up with you.

If she doesn't snuggle up, don't allow yourself to feel upset.

Instead relax and be cool. Just pull your arm back so that it's no longer touching her (but is still behind her on the top of the couch) and then try again later. Eventually, her horniness will have reached the point where she's dying to have your arm around her.

Hold hands. Put your arm around her. Stroke her silky hair, enjoying the feel of it running through your fingers. Sniff her hair sensually.

Do various things that the two of you have done thus far.

In fact, keep in mind the following parts of her body that... although they're "Rated PG"... are in reality erogenous zones:

1. **Her Hair.** Absolutely the best way to heat a woman up is to touch her hair.
2. Touch her **scalp** as well, since that's erogenous.
3. **The inside of her elbows.** The touch of your fingertips might make her shiver.
4. **The skin between her fingers.** When you hold hands with a woman, the best way to do it is to interlock fingers with hers.
5. **Her ears.** As you're getting close to kissing her, lightly blow into her ears. Touch the rims of her ears and her earlobes with your fingertips.
6. **Her shoulders.**
7. **Her feet.**
8. **Her toes.**

Touch the above areas, and she'll get increasingly aroused.

As things get more and more heated, move your face toward her hair and inhale deeply. Say, "Mmmmm I love the way your hair smells!"

As the interaction heats up more and more beyond you having your arms around her, the two of you will be gazing very deeply into each other's eyes, perhaps with mouths slightly open. At this point, ever so slightly brush your lower lip against hers, and watch her melt into a kiss with you.

Let your kissing progress; don't just jam your tongue into her mouth. Wait for her to give you a little bit of tongue, and then reciprocate. Pretty soon the two of you will be kissing passionately.

The "Rate My Kiss" Technique

Are you feeling too nervous about kissing a girl for the first time to go for it as directly as I've just described?, you can also go into it indirectly mention it, using what I like to call the "Rate Your Kiss" Technique.

Here's how the "Rate Your Kiss" Technique works. When you feel like the mood is right for the kiss, you say, "How would you rate your kissing ability on a scale of 1 to 10?"

She may answer or she may not, but at that point 95+% of the time the woman will open her lips and you can move your face towards hers.

The Non-Verbal Sign That Screams, "KISS ME!"

Other than that technique, there is a big non-verbal signal to look for that says, "Kiss me now, my dream man!"

The technique in a nutshell is this...

As you move your face and lips very close to hers (after having already inhaled the scent of her hair and so on), watch for her to slightly part her lips and have them go soft. Usually a woman will also close her eyes, though not always.

When you move in, concentrate not on kissing her, but on brushing your lips against hers. Trust me, she'll melt into you and the two of you will be kissing full-on in no time.

Kiss for awhile, slowly. Have your mouth open. Wait for her tongue. Once the tip of her tongue enters your mouth, match what she does.

The Most Important Thing for You to Know About Kissing

Kissing differs from many other sexual activities in that it's one of the few things that you do with a woman in which you should let her take the lead. When it comes to activities such as eating her out and penetrating her, you should take the lead. But again, not with kissing.

One of the biggest mood-killers for a woman is when a guy jams his tongue into her mouth before she's ready. So just relax during the kissing and mirror what she does.

The Alpha Method of Moving From First-Kiss to Home Plate

By now, not only are you making out with the woman, you're also hugging her and able to touch all parts of her back.

Remember, keep progressing slowly. The whole process usually takes a number of hours from when you first go through the door location until you're having sex.

Slowly take her shirt off. Unbutton one button, and then go back to kissing her. Think "Two steps forward, one step backward." Unbutton a 2nd button, and then go back to massaging her hand as you sniff her neck. Then stroke her hair.

Then touch her stomach slightly, and then move back to an earlier stage such as French kissing.

When you go for her breasts, do it slowly. Graze them slightly with your palms, and then move backwards into something else, like rubbing her stomach.

Eventually, she'll have her shirt all the way off and be in her bra. Slowly you'll want to put your hands under her bra.

Once you're fully comfortable touching her breasts, take off her bra. Then after going back to an earlier stage for a while (French kiss her, etc.), start sucking on her breasts and nipples.

Once you've reached 2nd base (i.e., sucking her breasts), your goal is now 3rd base (i.e., going down on her). With most women, once you are performing oral sex, you are virtually assured to be able to put your penis in.

Some women are fully conscious of that fact, so they will put up token resistance after you've started fingering her clitoris and just when you're ready to start eating her pussy.

A playboy friend of mine told me about a novel solution to this problem, which I have tested myself and found to work. He tells women that he "can't get it up tonight" and then points to his flaccid penis. "See how soft I am? All I want to do is eat you out," he says.

Then, while eating her out, he strokes his penis to make it hard. At this point, because the woman has been driven to orgasmic heights from the oral sex, she's practically pleading to have him make love to her. So… he does!

This brings up the issue of overcoming a woman's token resistance in general. Sometimes when you're moving too fast through foreplay, a woman will say things like, "We shouldn't be doing this" or "I don't want to go too far tonight."

A lot of guys will screw up the dynamic by getting disturbed and arguing with her. It is important that you not fall into this trap. Instead, disarm her by saying things like:

- "You're right, we shouldn't be doing this."

- "Okay, we won't go too far. It's nice what we've done already."
- "I have limits too."
- "You're right, we shouldn't have this much pleasure on the first night."

Once you've verbally disarmed her by agreeing with her, go back to what you've already done in earlier parts of the seduction, and then continue slowly escalating.

If you go slow enough and keep steadily persisting, gradually one barrier after another falls.

For example, suppose her shirt is off but her bra is still on, and you've been massaging her breasts from the outside of the fabric. Then, as you start to unfasten her bra, you hear, "This is too much for the first night."

"You're right, this is too much," you reply. "We'll just do what we've done so far."

At this point, go back a few steps. Massage her lower back, stroke her hair, kiss her, hold her close.

Gradually escalate, and then after awhile, as you're again massaging her breasts, do them so sensually and slowly and for so long that she will then put up no resistance to you taking off her bra.

By the way, when it comes to the final penetration, make sure to differentiate between token resistance and real resistance. If a woman says, "No!" then stop what you're doing.

If you force a woman to have sex, then you have committed the crime of rape. It is crucially important that you bear this in mind. Stop when she says no, but at the same time keep persisting towards the lay until you either get laid or have her **seriously** tell you to stop.

But in any event, don't chicken out by having her take the lead. (You're the man and are expected to be active).   Make sure to always lead the interaction. Be persistent.

By the way, be careful with condoms. The sight of a Trojan wrapper in your hand can snap a woman out of her horny state by triggering that portion of her brain that's been programmed to think sex is "bad."

It's important to use condoms, however, in order to be safe from disease and pregnancy, so try to put on your condom fast, without making a big scene out of it.

What I do is put on the condom while I'm eating the woman out (and she's too distracted to notice what I'm doing with my hands), so that when she's ready for me to enter her, everything goes smoothly.

CHAPTER 19: The Morning After

To prevent a woman from getting buyer's remorse, you need to call her after a night of passion.

By buyer's remorse, I'm referring to that sick feeling you get after a pushy salesman at the electronics store cons you into paying $200 for a warranty you'll never use. A lot of women get that, too, if they think they were just being used for a one night stand. They also feel guilty.

Often, all a woman will want is in fact a one-night stand. Although women talk a good game when it comes to men being the only ones interested in such things, it's been my experience that women love flings that have no strings attached, perhaps even more than we men do.

Why? Because women put a lot of emotional investment in relationships. When they get the opportunity for no-strings-attached sex, without social consequences, they often go for it.

It's up to you, the morning after, to decide what you want. If you want to pursue a relationship with the woman, then having passionate sex from the first day the two you dated is the ideal frame for it to get started. It sets up a dynamic within your relationship that sex is goes with everything and happens often.

Personally, I'm a big fan of relationships. I have standards and won't have sex with just any woman. And if I do go all the way with a woman who meets my standards, why have sex with her only once? Why would I not want to **keep on** having sex with her?

If you don't want to pursue a relationship, you can still keep things on a casual "fuck buddy" basis between the two of you.

To do this successfully, make sure to meet her no more than once per week to avoid having her see you as anything more than a sex partner. Any more than once a week, and she will start seeing you as a potential boyfriend.

In the odd case that you never want to see her again (maybe the sex was really bad?), at least have the decency to call her to check up on her.

CHAPTER 20: Being Dominant in a Group

A lot of other seduction methods talk a lot about picking up women in groups (and in fact, some of the nightclub methods are *based* on working groups).

I don't talk a lot about being in groups in this book, because the bottom line (in my opinion), is that you should only be in a group with a chick's friends AFTER you've fucked her. And at that point, as long as you remained chilled out, you've got nothing to be concerned about.

Having said that, however, here a few simple pointers to be an alpha male in an group situation...

1. **Always be the most relaxed person**, no matter what the group situation is. If someone else is affecting your reality, then they have dominance over you.

2. **Be talkative**. It literally does not matter what you're talking about... just keep those gums flapping. DON'T ANALYZE ANYTHING. Save all self-reflection until LATER. Just let your mind flow, and keep talking.

3. **Let nothing affect your reality**. If someone says something to get a rise out of you, don't allow it.

Mainly just follow those three things, and you'll ALWAYS remain alpha. (You may not always be at the very top of every group, because hey, what if the President's in your group? But you'll at least be near the top, and that's all that matters.)

Notice something about those three rules? They're all INTERNAL. Just have your internals in order, and you'll do fine in group situations. There's no need to have any material memorized or to make a big deal about any mechanics.

As you're being talkative in a group, don't just recite memorized comedy material like the advice around the net sometimes tells you to do, because unless you become VERY GOOD at spouting routines, it'll come across at best as you being their **entertainment monkey**, and at worst as you looking like a **weirdo on drugs**.

Just be the alpha male and talk about whatever you've got on your mind at the time, and you'll always be okay in group settings.

Besides those three rules, the same guidelines apply for groups as for the one-on-one situations that I've talked about earlier. You should feel free to enter other people's space, only talk about the things that actually interest you, don't smile unless there's something to smile about, etc.

As far as eye contact with men in your group (or men in general, by the way), my question is, who cares? It's truly irrelevant what other guys think of you.

The only time you should make eye contact w/ a guy is when you're saying something to him. When the other guy is talking, don't look at him much, instead looking off to the side. (Ever dealt with a CEO? That's exactly what they do when it comes to eye contact.)

Most importantly, when picking up a girl who's with her friends, **try to get a girl by herself and away from the group**. For a woman to become horny, she needs to feel relaxed and low-energy. The problem with groups is that they're high energy, which is the very opposite of how you want a woman to feel.

CHAPTER 21: Some General Relationship Advice

An entire book could be written on how to have a successful relationship by being an alpha male. (And in fact... I plan to write such a book!)

In order to have sex with a girl in the first place, you need to establish your dominant frame. So having done that, in order to have a good relationship, all you need to do is to keep your dominant frame.

The main way to do that, I've found, is to apply the concept I call **punishment and reward**. Simply put, you reward good behavior and punish bad behavior.

If your girlfriend does something you like, then reward her with more of your attention. If she does something you don't, then punish her by withdrawing your attention.

So many guys do the opposite... when their woman behaves badly (e.g., by saying, "not tonight"), they actually REWARD that behavior by cuddling up with her all night.

Make sure to draw the line and not put up with bad behavior. If you're consistent about it, her bad behavior will cease. And if she knows you'll be nice to her when she has earned it, she'll act in ways that cause you to reward her.

The ultimate key to success with line drawing is to always be genuinely ready to walk out at any given moment. Not that you will walk out… but that if your girlfriend knows she has to work to keep you, she will (and also, she'll love you more for it).

Avoid any sort of low-status behaviors like arguing with your girlfriend. And certainly never insult her. The best way to do this is to visualize it is as if you're the big man who's protecting her (almost as if you're her father).

By the way, it's important to women to feel like you're the big man keeping them safe when they're in your arms. In fact, lots of women may even say things like, "I feel so safe" when you hold them.

Doing gentlemanly things for her helps create the impression of you being the strong man. Open doors for her in an alpha fashion. (Have the mindset that you're stronger than she is, not that you're trying to win her affections.) Walk on the outside of the sidewalk, so that you're the one nearest the street.

Be the alpha male. Respect yourself, and she'll respect you too. There's never any need to defend yourself or explain yourself. Your relationship is a great thing, and will remain that way as long as you remain happy in it.

Even though the relationship is a wonderful thing, it's best if your girlfriend detects that it could all disappear at the drop of a hat. That keeps everything a challenge for her.

Women love to chase a man, so allow her to chase you. The man's responsibility is for the sex, not the relationship. You make sure you get lots of sex (or else leave her for other girls), and in turn let her do the work when it comes to the relationship.

So you can relax a lot of the time and let her do the work. Let her be the one to call you to set up get-togethers. Don't feel like you have to call her that often.

If she chases you, then she will value you more. It's a simple fact of human psychology.

It is often said, so much so that it's almost a cliche, that "whoever cares least controls the relationship." I think I first read that axiom in a relationship book written in the 1970s.

It may be a cliche, but that's because there's so much truth to it. Let the woman think that she care more about the relationship than you do. Don't always jump to do things for her.

With that said, however, make sure that your girlfriend knows you appreciate what she does. That way she'll feel rewarded for her good behavior.

Say things like, "Thank you for cooking dinner for me tonight baby. It was so good! You're the best!"

Also tell her things such as, "You please me." Not only does hearing "you please me" make her feel good, but it is also a command in a way. Your girlfriend will want to continue to do the things required to please you.

Basically, the ideal scenario to be in is one in which the woman thinks she's putting a lot of investment into the relationship and that investment is paying off nicely. That way, you stay in control of the relationship.

So, although it's best to always let her do more of the work, you can (and should) do things for her.

Give her unexpected small gifts. They should not be expensive, because the woman might then resent the fact that you're trying to "buy" her affections (which means you're no longer a challenge for her).

Make sure to put time and thought into the gifts. One strategy for this is to listen for things that she says she likes. If she tells you she likes a particular song, for example, then surprise her with a CD of the band.

A woman needs surprises and spontaneity in her life. One of the best ways to kill a relationship is to make it predictable.

Pick a random day of the month and buy her flowers on that day. Take surprise trips. Go on surprise dinner outings.

You can accelerate the process of your girlfriend falling in love with you by talking about "destiny" with her. Even though your good relationship is really sustained by you affecting the behaviors and mindset of an alpha male, don't tell her that.

Instead let her live out her life-long fantasies through you. The vast majority of women want to "embrace" their destiny with a man whom they consider their soul mate. So talk freely about how destiny has brought the two of you together!

When building up to the L-Bomb ("I love you") don't just blurt out that phrase. You'll have more success (and keep more control of the relationship) if you remain a challenge for awhile. Use the words "I adore you" a few months before finally saying "I love you."

Finally, don't devote yourself 100% to any woman. Have other interests in your life that pull you away from her from time to time.

CHAPTER 22: Conclusion

As you take control of your thoughts and attitude and go for your dreams in life, you will find that you're becoming genuinely happy in a way that you've never felt before.

With women, you'll be so successful and attractive that you never have to do anything other than just be yourself to get sex.

I'll recap by restating a truly amazing psychological technique I've talked about throughout this guide... proven through decades of completely scientific research on my part. (I've dated over a thousand women in the past two and a half decades and had sex with more than a hundred.)

The technique is so simple... yet massively effective and nearly impossible for most guys to figure out on their own, because they engage in too damn much self-analysis.

The technique is simply this:

1) Don't self-analyze at all when you're with a woman. Just keep your mind focused on what comes naturally.
2) Maintain the dominant frame in all your dealings.
3) Control your own perceptions of reality

Just do the above three things, and you will achieve the dreams that used to be your wildest fantasies. In fact, you'll literally be able to make any woman dripping wet for you... with just your mind!

Truly be yourself. Share yourself and get to know women. Do what you want with them... be romantic, have sex, whatever.

Remember: You're in this life to enjoy yourself and be happy. Not tomorrow, but today.

Finally, keep this in mind. With this guide, you've learned everything you need to know to become an alpha male. Now it's your turn. It's time to **apply what you've** learned.

Just reading and learning does little for you unless you also use what you've learned.

So get out there and do it! I promise you'll have spectacular success rising above and beyond what you thought possible. There's no doubt in my mind about that.

Thank you for purchasing this guide. If you have any questions, please email me. As a purchaser, you're entitled to 12 free, private email consultations with me, so keep in touch. I am here for you.

Your friend,

John Alexander

John Alexander
July 15, 2005

Other Books By John Alexander

How to be Her Best Lover Ever - A sex guide for men that will have you giving your woman sex so good, she'll beg you for more. Available at http://www.herbestlover.com

Books Published By John Alexander Enterprises and Edited by John Alexander

Developing Your Male Charisma - Become a leader of men and romancer of women through your charm and new-found interpersonal skills. Make easy conversations and become a master at building deep connections. Available at http://www.malecharisma.com

Printed in the United Kingdom
by Lightning Source UK Ltd.
134678UK00002B/100/A